A LENTEN JOURNEY

with Jesus Christ and

ST. JOHN _{OF THE} CROSS

An Invitation of Grace,

a Prayer of Hope,

and a Gift of Peace.

A LENTEN JOURNEY
with *Jesus Christ* and
ST. JOHN OF THE CROSS

Daily Gospel Readings

with

Selections from the Writings

of

St. John of the Cross

REFLECTIONS AND PRAYERS

BY

REV. GEORGE MANGIARACINA, O.C.D.

WITH ADDITIONAL INTRODUCTORY MATERIAL BY

PETER J. MONGEAU

WELLESLEY, MA

www.ChristusPublishing.com

Christus Publishing, LLC
Wellesley, Massachusetts
www.ChristusPublishing.com

Rev. George Mangiaracina, O.C.D. has been a Discalced Carmelite friar since 1988 with the Discalced Carmelites of the Washington Province. He was ordained into the priesthood in 1993. He earned a Licentiate degree in Sacred Liturgy in 2001, and his doctorate degree in Sacred Liturgy from Sant' Anselmo College in Rome, Italy in 2008. He is a conventual member of the Monastery of the Espousal of Mary and Joseph in Brighton, MA.

Peter J. Mongeau is the Founder and Publisher of Christus Publishing, LLC.

Publisher's Cataloging-in-Publication Data
Mangiaracina, George.
  A Lenten Journey with Jesus Christ and St. John of the Cross : daily Gospel readings with selections from the writings of St. John of the Cross : reflections and prayers / by George Mangiaracina ; with additional introductory material by Peter J. Mongeau.

  p. ; cm.

  Includes bibliographical references.
  ISBN: 978-0-9841707-2-2

1. Lent--Prayers and devotions. 2. John of the Cross, Saint, 1542-1591.
3. John of the Cross, Saint, 1542-1591--Prayers and devotions. 4. Catholic Church--Prayers and devotions. 5. Carmelites--Prayers and devotions.
6. Prayer books. I. Mongeau, Peter J. II. Title.

BX2170.L4 M36 2009

242/.34   2009938837

Printed and bound in the United State of America

10 9 8 7 6 5 4 3 2 1

Text design and layout by Peri Swan
This book was typeset in Garamond Premier Pro with Snell Roundhand as a display typeface

CONTENTS

ACKNOWLEDGMENTS

The Gospel passages are taken from the *Lectionary for Mass for Use in the Dioceses of the United States of America, second typical edition* © 2001, 1998, 1997, 1986, 1970 Confraternity of Christian Doctrine, Inc., Washington, DC. Used with permission. All rights reserved. No portion of this text may be reproduced by any means without permission in writing from the copyright owner.

The citations from St. John of the Cross are from *The Collected Works of St. John of the Cross,* revised edition, translated by Kieran Kavanaugh, O.C.D. and Otilio Rodriguez, O.C.D. © 1991 Washington Province of Discalced Carmelite Friars, Inc. Published by ICS Publications, Washington, DC, 1991. Reprinted with permission.

Reflections and prayers © 2009 Christus Publishing, LLC.

ABBREVIATIONS

A=Ascent of Mount Carmel; N=Dark Night; C=Spiritual Canticle; CO=Counsels to a Religious; F=Living Flame; P=Poetry; S=Sayings of Light and Love; Pr=Precautions; L=Letters

Periods separate levels of division: book, chapter, paragraph number (e.g., A 3.27.5); or stanza, paragraph number (e.g., C 10.1). En-dashes separate inclusive numbers (e.g., N 1.9.5–6) and lowercase letters indicate paragraph levels within a citation (e.g., 15.10c–e).

AN INVITATION
FROM
ST. JOHN
OF THE CROSS

"Where have you hidden,
Beloved, and left me moaning?
you fled like the stag
after wounding me;
I went out calling you, but you were gone" (Collected Works, 471).

With these lines from the first stanza of the Spiritual Canticle, John of the Cross describes a soul touched by God, who is longing to find him yet she cannot. He describes the soul as someone who has become aware that she was created for a higher good, and that she needs to undergo a conversion in order to do so.

---

1. The citation is from *The Collected Works of St. John of the Cross,* trans. Kieran Kavanaugh, O.C.D. and Otilio Rodriguez, O.C.D. (Washington, DC: ICS Publications, 1991). Hereafter, *Collected Works.*

"In this first stanza the soul, enamored of the Word, her Bridegroom, the Son of God, longs for union with him through clear and essential vision. She records her longings of love and complains to him of his absence, especially since his love wounds her. Through this love she went out from all creatures and from herself, and yet she must suffer her Beloved's absence, for she is not freed from mortal flesh as the enjoyment of him in the glory of eternity requires." (Collected Works, 478).

As the Season of Lent is a call to conversion through prayer, fasting, and almsgiving, John of the Cross, with his added insistence on conversion, is a good guide for the Season of Lent. For John of the Cross, conversion takes place when God calls the faithful to replace their usual way of finding fulfillment in life, with God himself. As John of the Cross says in book one of the Ascent,

"God, then, with compassion for all those who through such labor and cost to themselves strive to satisfy the thirst and hunger of their appetites for creatures, proclaims through Isaiah: "All you that thirst, come to the waters: and you that have no money make haste, buy, and eat: come ye, buy wine and milk without money, and without any price" [Is 55:1–2, translation of the original Latin text]"(*Collected Works,* 134).

Thus, with the guidance of John of the Cross, Lent can become a period of renewal, a period where we reorder our priorities from many things to one: God alone. We still have our work to do and obligations to fulfill, but throughout Lent we can learn to be for God alone and to find our reward in God alone.

Such an undertaking cannot be done by mere human willing; we need the help of God, which comes primarily through prayer. Lent and prayer go together like labor and energy. Without the energy that comes from food, we would have a hard time getting our labor done. The same is true with ordering our lives around God during Lent. Without the energy that comes from encountering God in prayer, we will not have

---

2. "This saying comes from the Cathrusian Guigo II's *Scala paradisi*, ch. 2, in Migne, PL 40. 998," *Collected Works,* 97, n. 11.

the energy to center our lives around God alone, much like Elijah could not continue the journey to Mount Horeb unless he ate the food given to him by an angel. Like Elijah, and in the words of John of the Cross, *"Seek in reading and you will find in meditation; knock in prayer and it will be opened to you in contemplation."*

We can see that prayer is seeking God from the heart in one's spirit in order to commune with him who is pure spirit. As Jesus told the Samaritan woman, *God is Spirit, and those who worship him must worship in Spirit and truth* (Jn 4:24). Thus, we must seek God in our spirit, created in his image and likeness, so that we can commune with Him who is spirit.

The book consists of the Gospel of the day, a brief introduction to the extract taken from the works of John of the Cross, the extract itself; and a prayer. You can begin with any one of these as it helps you. One thing to keep in mind is a word that John of the Cross uses that is often misunderstood is the word "appetite." He does not mean by this word appetite for a meal. He means the inner desire for some form of gratification one gets from the pleasure in using people or things. It is this inordinate drive that takes possession of us and leaves us unfree to say "no" with which he is concerned. This force was called "concupiscence" in ancient times and later Freud called it the "id."

The purpose of this work, along with others in this series, is to introduce Catholics to the great spiritual authors of the past and to guide them in their journey through the twenty-first century. As will be seen in the following pages, John of the Cross is a good guide for the Season of Lent. His language is demanding because the road leading to God is demanding. He is like an old scout who has traveled this way before and offers us a friendly hand to guide us. We may find his way a little rugged at times, but we can be sure that if we follow his guidance, we will get to where we most want to be: united with God.

REV. GEORGE MANGIARACINA, O.C.D.

ST. JOHN
OF THE CROSS:
A SHORT
BIOGRAPHY

John of the Cross was born Juan de Yepes Alvarez in 1542 at Fontiveros, a small village near Avila in Spain. His mother was a poor seamstress and his father, though he came from a wealthy family, was forced to learn his wife's trade because his family disinherited him because he married outside his class. Even after the father's death, his family would not support his wife or his children. Thus, the future John of the Cross entered life in a poor family with little prospects of becoming well-to-do.

In 1551, his mother took her three boys to Medina del Campo where she took up her seamstress trade. During this time, one of her three boys died, possibly from hunger or malnutrition. She tried to train her son John to be a seamstress too, but he did not have a hand for it, nor other manual trades at that time. He did show a gift for reading and caring for the sick and with these he was able to help in a nearby hospital and take courses in reading and writing. He even had a chance to become the hospital's chaplain, which gave a good income. However, he turned it down. No answer has ever been supplied as to why he did so; but it shows that even at this young age, he was leaning toward the more challenging rather than to the easier. As he would say in his book of the Ascent:

"Endeavor to be inclined always:
    not to the easiest, but to the most difficult;
    not to the most delightful, but to the most distasteful;
    not to the most gratifying, but to the less pleasant;
    not to what means rest for you, but to hard work;
    not to the consoling, but to the unconsoling;
    not to the most, but to the least;
    not to the highest and most precious, but to the lowest and most despised;
    not to wanting something, but to wanting nothing.
    Do not go about looking for the best of temporal things, but for the worst, and, for Christ, desire to enter into complete nakedness, emptiness, and poverty in everything in the world" (Collected Works, 149).

Thus, even at an early age, he was well on his way to becoming the man of God that we see today. He chose to join the Order of Carmelites, possibly because the order is dedicated to Mary. In any case, he entered its novitiate in 1563 at Medina and took the name Fray (Brother) John of St. Matthias. Shortly thereafter, he went to school to study philosophy and then theology at Salamanca.

Even as a novice and later as a professed Carmelite, he showed signs of wanting to live the rule of his order more faithfully. So much so that when Teresa of Avila came to Medina del Campo in 1567 to find friars to help her with the reform of Carmelite nuns that she had begun in 1562, the future John of the Cross' name was given to her. John, who was about twenty-five, was also in Medina del Campo to celebrate his ordination to the priesthood. At the time, Teresa of Avila was old enough to be his mother.

When she met with John, she found in him a willing helper, but also an impatient one. He was thinking of joining the Carthusians at the time and he told her to be quick about getting the reform going for the friars as well. When Teresa later wrote about finding some friars to join her cause, she wrote, I found a friar-and-a-half (the half being John, who was short.) Later Teresa would write of him, he might be small, but I am sure he is big in the eyes of God. The other friar was Antonio de Jesús de Heredia whom Teresa was not too sure about given his age. He will be the same friar who comes to John of the Cross' support twenty-four years later.

In 1572, Teresa took John of the Cross with her to Avila to help her with her work with the nuns at the Monastery of the Incarnation where she had begun her life as a Carmelite. Many of the nuns were afraid she would impose her ideal on them, but she told them that she had no such intention and that it was Mary of Carmel who was the real prioress.

John of the Cross was her spiritual director during this time, and the chaplain to the nuns. It was also during this time that Teresa of Jesus underwent her spiritual marriage and began her most fruitful period in prayer and in response to her calling to find other monasteries of nuns.

John of the Cross, on the other hand, stayed behind to continue his work of being the nuns' chaplain when a group of Carmelite friars came and kidnapped him in December 1577. They were jealous of the success that he and other Carmelites of the Reformed (initially called Contemplative Carmelites but later called Discalced Carmelites) were having; and they wanted to break John in order to end Teresa's movement for the friars as well.

This was a very difficult time for both Catholics and religious. It is the early stages of the Counter-Reformation, and in Spain there was a great deal of suspicion over who was for or against the Church. It was also a period when the king and the pope were involved with the welfare of the order. To rectify matters, there was a chapter convened in Piacenza, Italy in May 1575. This chapter held that all foundations founded in Andulusia without approval of the legitimate superiors were to be closed. Later, when John of the Cross refused to renounce his commitment to the reformed friars under obedience, he was severely punished by imprisonment and lashed in public before the friars. The reason he did not submit was he felt that the chapter acts (that were read to him) did not apply to him as he was at the Incarnation by the order of the papal nuncio Nicolás Ormaneto.

However, it was in this period that John of the Cross grew in holiness; or at least, he allowed his sufferings to make him holier than he was. He was put in a small room, just barely large enough to hold him; and he was fed on bread and water. From time to time, the friars would come by his cell and talk about the end of the Carmelite reform. When the feast of the Blessed Virgin Mary came out, he was refused the right to celebrate Mass, which caused him to cry.

Around August of 1578, he realized that the Carmelite Friars were not going to let him go. He spent a few days, possibly weeks, thinking about making his escape, which he accomplished on August 15 by getting out of the monastery with the help of a rope he had put together. His rope was short by several feet, so he jumped and hurt his leg when he landed. There is a plaque put up by the city of Toledo to mark the spot where he landed. It did not take long for the friars to find out and he had to hide in the Carmelite nuns' monastery. Later, they got him to a hospital and later he rejoined his group of Discalced Carmelite Friars. Since he was still being sought, he went to the Andalusian province where he remained until the end of his life.

While he was in prison, he wrote poems that he shared with the nuns who in turn asked him for a commentary on them. That is how we have his books. For about ten years, he lived a quiet life fulfilling various offices given to him by the friars of the reform. He was a prior of the house in Granada, and a confessor for the nuns in Ubeda. Then, in 1590, he ran afoul of the new general of the order, Doria, who had been a businessman from Italy before he joined the friars. He wanted to have greater control over the nuns, but when John of the Cross opposed him because it was not in the spirit of Teresa of Avila, Doria became very angry at him and had him stripped of all his offices. To make matters worse, he also supported a persecution drive by Juan Evangelista who sought to embarrass John of the Cross and get him thrown out of the order.

Also at this time, John of the Cross became ill and he had a choice of going to two convents: one where he would be treated fairly, and another where he would be poorly treated. Following his own teaching of doing what is more difficult, he went to the monastery where he would be poorly treated. This convent was in Ubeda, and when he got there, the prior, Fray Francisco Crisóstomo, did not want to have anything to do with him, and told him he was a drain on the finances of the house. John of the Cross received this treatment meekly and did not complain or put up a fuss. The only thing he asked for was to die in his habit.

By 1591, Antonio, the other friar with Teresa of Avila back in 1566, had become vicar provincial, and when he heard where John of the Cross was and how he was being treated, he went over there to give him support. Antonio even had a music band come over and entertain him. John of the Cross thanked them but asked them not to trouble themselves over him.

Then, nearing the end on December 14, 1591, he said that he will be saying his matins in heaven. At this time, John of the Cross invited the prior to see him and forgive him for all the trouble he caused. The prior realized that John of the Cross was a holy man and begged his forgiveness. After this experience, it was remarked that the prior went on to become a holy man. John of the Cross breathed his last and legend has it that a white sphere left his body when he died.

Except for his periods of persecution in 1577 and 1591, there is not much that is remarkable about the life of this man. All that he did was work on denying his desires for any physical and personal gratification with the help of God through prayer. By doing so, he grew in charity in helping out those in need and forgiving those who had harmed him. He never spoke badly of the friars who jailed him in 1577 or became bitter. For him, they were the tool of God chiseling away at his self-love to make room for God in him. His attitude about them can be seen in the letter he wrote to a nun while undergoing his second persecution:

"Do not let what is happening to me, daughter, cause you any grief, for it does not cause me any. What greatly grieves me is that one who is not at fault is blamed. Men do not do these things, but God, who knows what is suitable for us and arranges things for our own good. Think nothing else but that God ordains all, and where there is no love, put love, and you will draw out love" (Collected Works, 760).

When I was studying Spanish in Granada, Spain, my tutor told me that he was a unique man in an extraordinary time in the history of Spain. Even today, he is as much a challenge to read for the Spaniards as he is for us. He was a unique man, a holy man, in an extraordinary age.

REV. GEORGE MANGIARACINA, O.C.D.

ORDER OF CARMELITES DISCALCED: A BRIEF HISTORY

Unlike the Benedictines, Franciscans, or Dominicans, the Carmelite order does not have a specific founder. Also, it does not have a specific date as to when it was founded. Rather, it focuses on where it was founded, and who inspired its founding: Mount Carmel, and the prophet Elijah. Carmelites see themselves as the spiritual sons of Elijah.

As far as we know, the Carmelite order was founded in 1209 AD when they were given a rule by Albert, the Patriarch of Jerusalem; although when he gave the rule for the order the patriarchy was actually in Acre because the Turks were occupying Jerusalem. Albert seems to have made his rule in consultation with the hermits living on Mount Carmel. Albert was the Patriarch of Jerusalem from 1206 to 1214 (thus the approximate date of the rule). He was killed in a procession by a man who was upset with him over not getting a job. Perhaps this is why Carmelites do not like the idea of getting too attached to their desires.

As the Crusades began to meet with failure, over the years, groups of Carmelite hermits made their way back to Europe. One group of hermits to be taken back into Western Europe were those brought over by King Louis IX after he completed his four-year stint in the Levant trying to recapture Jerusalem in 1254. He did not succeed and he planned to try again a second time in 1270, by approaching via North Africa. On his way to the Holy Land, he died in Tunis from the plague and never achieved his dream. To paraphrase St. Francis de Sales, God gives people inspirations to do great things in his service but not necessarily great results in order to keep them humble.

By 1290, most, if not all, the hermit friars had fled Mount Carmel to escape the persecution of the Saracens. Legend has it that the last ones killed on Mount Carmel were singing the Salve Regina. Like many stories surrounding the order, this is probably a myth.

The transition of the hermits into Western Europe was not easy. Pope Innocent IV asked a pair of Dominicans to look over the rule and change it to that of a mendicant order instead of a monastic one. At the time, there were many monastic orders in Europe so the reasoning was there was no need for another one. Another possible reason for this choice was that the hermits on Mount Carmel arose out of the mendicant movement that flourished in the twelfth century, which was comprised of hermits who wanted to go to the Holy Land in support of the Second Crusade (1148–1149) encouraged by the preaching of St. Bernard of Clairvaux.[1]

With this newly revised rule of 1247, the mendicant Carmelite order began to flourish. St. Simon Stock (d. 1265) is usually credited with making this adjustment successful.[2] Legend has it that Mary appeared

---

1. Geoffrey Hindley, *The Crusades: Islam and Christianity in the Struggle for World Supremacy* (New York: Carroll & Graf, 2004) 2, 72. It is often overlooked that St. Bernard preached that the war against the Turks would be won more by fasting and prayer rather than relying on weapons. This same sentiment would be expressed by St. Teresa of Avila when she taught that the struggle against Protestantism would be won more by resorting to prayer than by the power of the state.

2. Peter-Thomas Rohrback, *Journey to Carith: The Sources and Story of the Discalced Carmelites* (Washington, DC: ICS Publications, 1966), 67. Hereafter, *Story of the Discalced Carmelites*.

to him and gave him the scapular the Carmelites wear today. Whether the legend is true or not, it did continue the bond with Mount Carmel where the frairs had a chapel built in honor of her.

There was some opposition to this change led by a general of the order, Nicholas the Frenchman, in his letter to the order called the *Fiery Arrow,* written around 1270; but for the most part, since vocations were increasing, there was little opposition.

But in the 1300s a crisis arose as to how to explain the order to the novices. In 1379, Felip Ribot wrote *Institutes of the First Monks* in which he drew on the life of Elijah as a model for the friars.[3] This worked out well for awhile; but then came the Black Death which greatly reduced the number of monks and religious in Europe, including Carmelites, so they petitioned Pope Eugene IV in 1432 to modify their rule a second time and this was granted.[4]

During this time, they suffered like other religious orders over the Great Schism that divided the Catholic world, even the religious orders. When the schism ended, the parties were reunited at which point the challenge became successfully returning to the premodified rule of 1247. Two Carmelite Generals John Soreth (d. 1471) and Nicholas Audet (d. 1526) tried to return the order to its earlier discipline but with little success.[5]

It was from an unlikely source that the reform of the Carmelites would come: Teresa of Avila, also known as Teresa of Jesus. She was born in 1515 at Avila, Spain; and she entered the Incarnation convent when she was twenty. After about a year, she suffered what we would call a nervous breakdown and had to leave. During her period of recovering, she stayed at her uncle's who had a large collection of books on spirituality. After her recovery, she returned to the convent of the Incarnation

---

3. Richard Copsey, *The Ten Books on the Way of Life and Great Deeds of the Carmelites* (including the *Book of the First Monks,* a medieval history of the Carmelites written c. 1385 by Felip Ribot), ed. and trans. Richard Copsey (Faversham, Kent, UK: Saint Albert's Press, 2005), ix-xi.

4. *Story of the Discalced Carmelites,* 111.

5. *Story of the Discalced Carmelites,* 117.

and renewed her life there. During this time, she heard of the Protestant Reformation, and she thought that if there was to be any success against this movement breaking up the Church, she would have to live out her vows more perfectly. She also underwent a conversion around 1554 when she saw a statue of our Lord overcome with wounds. At the sight of this statue, she fell down and prayed. She was granted her prayer, and she began a reform of the Carmelite nuns by starting another community in Avila under the title of St. Joseph. From there she continued to find other communities picking up St. John of the Cross and other friars along the way. By the time she died in 1581, she had founded fifteen monasteries throughout Spain; and her daughters would go on to found monasteries in France and the Netherlands.

From her reform movement, eventually came two branches of the Carmelite Order: the original group called the Order of Carmelites (also known as "of the Ancient Observance" (O. Carm.) and the new group called the Discalced Carmelites (also known as "of the Primitive Observance" (O.C.D.). Each one went its own way and they remain independent orders to this day.

While Teresa of Jesus made headway with her reform, the Carmelites of the Ancient Observance also made their reform called the Reform of Touraine in the seventeenth century. It was characterized by having a strong conventual discipline and led to "a more active and organized apostolate."[6]

With the call of the Church to renew herself in the light of Vatican II, the two orders have started to dialogue and search for ways to work with each other. The products of this effort are a common calendar to be used with the celebration of the liturgy, and a new dictionary on the spirituality and history of the order. There is a dynamism inherent in the order that keeps pushing it to respond to God as Elijah once did, saying, "The Lord is God in whose presence I stand."

REV. GEORGE MANGIARACINA, O.C.D.

---

6. *Story of the Discalced Carmelites,* 228.

HISTORY
OF
LENT

The Season of Lent grew out of the celebration of the Feast of Easter, which in turn grew out of the celebration of Sunday as the Lord's Day. Christians valued this day sacramentally becuase they saw it as the day God created the earth, the day Jesus rose from the dead, and "the beginning of a new creation."[1] All four evangelists stress that Jesus rose on the "First Day"; and Luke in his Gospel connects the Day of Jesus' Resurrection with the Eucharist in his account of Jesus breaking bread with the disciples at Emmaus (Luke 24:34–53).

Then, turning to other New Testament references to the First Day, we see reference to the first day of the week in 1 Corinthians 16:1–2,

---

1. Eugene LaVerdiere, *The Eucharist in the New Testament and the Early Church.* (Collegeville, MN: The Liturgical Press, 1996), 109. Hereafter, Early Church.

Acts 20:7–12, and Revelation 1:9–10.[2] In the account from Acts we have what might be called a primitive form of the Mass in that it has a Liturgy of the Word (during which there was an interruption due to Eutychus falling off the window sill), the Breaking of the Bread, followed by another long discourse (what would today probably be the rest of the Eucharistic Prayer but in much shorter form).[3] In Revelation 1:9–10, we have the first reference to this day being the Lord's day.[4]

Some time between the years 90 and 100, the annual feast of Easter was established. There is no written account of the founding of Easter as an annual celebration. The earliest accounts of an annual Easter celebration date from the second century in present-day Turkey.[5] "The epistle of the Apostles, an apocryphal text written around the year 150; the homily On Easter by Melito of Sardis, from around the year 165; and the Holy Easter by an anonymous Quartodeciman from the end of the second century."[6] The Quartodecimans were those who celebrated the Feast of Easter on the fourteenth of Nisan. The reason for this was that Christians "were convinced that the death of Christ had been substituted for the Jewish Passover, the Pesach."[7] As a result of this group's insistence that the feast be celebrated on the fourteenth of Nisan a controversy arose with the pope in Rome who wanted the conclusion of the feast to be celebrated on Sunday, and not on any day the Passover of the Lord landed, which is what the Quartodecimans advocated. Around the year 190,[8] Pope Victor excommunicated all the

---

2. Scripture citations from Matias Augé, "The Liturgical Year in the First Four Centuries," in *Handbook for Liturgical Studies: Volume V, Liturgical Time and Space,* ed. Anscar J. Chupungco (Collegeville, MN: The Liturgical Press, 2000), 135–36. Hereafter, "The Liturgical Year."

3. *Early Church,* 109.

4. "The Liturgical Year," 136.

5. "The Liturgical Year," 146.

6. "The Liturgical Year," 148.

7. "The Liturgical Year," 146.

8. William A. Jurgens, *Faith of the Early Fathers* (Collegeville, MN: The Liturgical Press, 1970), 106.

Asian churches for not wanting to let go of their apostolic tradition. Irenaeus, however, in league with the other bishops of Gaul, wrote a letter to Pope Victor asking him to accept the difference in the name of peace and unity; and he reminded him that fifty years earlier Pope Anicetus and Polycarp argued over the same matter, but strove to maintain unity and peace over division.[9]

The important thing from the point of view of this study is that in this letter from Irenaeus, we have our first account of the length of the period of preparation for the Feast of Easter. According to Irenaeus, some had one day, others two, and still others forty hours.[10]

Going into the third century, we find more witnesses to the period of preparation. These concern not so much the time spent as who should be involved in this period of preparation, namely, catechumens. This development is witnessed to by Hippolytus[11] and Tertullian.[12]

It is in the fourth century that the preparation time for celebrating Easter extends to four weeks. This was witnessed to by the Council of Nicea (325), the letters of St. Athanasius to his flock back in Alexandria encouraging it to partake in this preparation of fasting before Easter,[13] a letter to Marcella from St. Jerome around the year 384 in which he records that this period of forty days is characterized by fasting.[14]

With the fifth century, the preparation period is extended to penitents who "were reconciled on the Thursday prior to Easter" according to Innocent I.[15] Along with this we have a further growth in the preach-

---

9. Cantalamessa, *Easter in the Early Church* (Collegeville, MN: The Liturgical Press, 1993), 33–37. Hereafter, Easter.

10. Easter, 36.

11. William Harmless, *Augustine and the Catechumenate* (Collegeville, MN: The Liturgical Press, 1995), 44.

12. E. Glenn Hinson, *The Church Triumphant: A History of Christianity Up to 1300* (Macon, GA: Mercer University Press, 1995), 57.

13. Alexander Schmemann, *Great Lent* (Crestwood, NY: St. Vladimir's Seminary Press, 1974), 135–37.

14. "The Liturgical Year," 183.

15. "The Liturgical Year," 184.

ing about the forty days of Lent from St. Leo the Great (d. 461).[16]

The growth of the preparation period before the celebration grows further in the sixth century with the addition of three more weeks before the period of forty days before Easter begins. These Sundays are called: Septuagesima, Sexagesima, and Quinquagesima Sundays.[17] It also becomes a period in which Christians do penance for their sins.[18] This group of Christians would eventually form into what would later be called the Order of Penitents.

Near the end of his pontificate, Gregory the Great (d. 604), makes the following reforms: he adds three days before Lent begins (this is where we would eventually get our Ash Wednesday, and the days preceding the First Sunday of Lent), and he suppresses the saying alleluia.[19] He also bears witness to the Roman custom of not eating "flesh, meat, and from all things that come from flesh, as milk, cheese and eggs in his letter to St. Augustine of Cantebury."[20] After his pontificate, a tendency developed in Rome to focus on the fasting dimension of Lent and no longer on the other two aspects: alms and prayer.[21]

Going into the eighth century there was only one minor reform made to the Season of Lent by Pope Gregory II (715–731) who gave

---

16. Irénée Henri Dalmais, Pierre Jounel, and Aimé Georges Martimort, *The Liturgy and Time,* vol. 4, trans. Matthew J. O'Connell (Collegeville, MN: The Liturgical Press, 1986), 66. *Eglise en prière.* English title, *The Church at Prayer: An Introduction to the Liturgy,* ed. Aimé Georges Martimort, intro.Gerard S. Sloyan (Collegeville, MN: The Liturgical Press, 1992).

17. "The Liturgical Year,"184.

18. Dom Gaspar LeFebvre, O.S.B., *Saint Andrew Daily Missal with Vespers for Sundays and Feasts* (Saint Paul: Lohmann, 1957), 192–95. Hereafter, *Saint Andrew Daily Missal.*

19. Mario Righetti, *Manuale di storia liturgica;* Terza Edizione (Milano: Àncora, 1969).Vol. II, L'Anno Liturgico, nella storia, nella messa, nell'ufficio (129) refers to Callewaert, *L'oeuvre liturgique de S. Gregoire,* in *Sacris erudiri,* 642.

20. Fr. William Saunders, History of Lent, available at http://www.catholiceducation.org/ articles/religion/re0527.html. See also Adolf Adam, *The Liturgical Year: Its History & Its Meaning after the Reform of the Liturgy,* trans. Matthew J. O'Connell (New York: Pueblo, 1981), 92, n. 68. Hereafter, *Reform.*

21. *Saint Andrew Daily Missal,* 195.

the Thursdays of Lent their own formulas for the celebration of the Eucharist. Prior to that time, there was no Mass on Thursdays during the Season of Lent.[22]

Several more centuries pass without any major changes to the Season of Lent; but with the end of the eleventh century, all the faithful will have ashes distributed to them "on the Wednesday before the first Sunday of Lent." This practice was prescribed by Urban II at the Synod of Benevento in 1091 in which he legislated that "both the clergy and laity" would receive ashes with a procession as we now have it on Ash Wednesday.[23] This development was in part due to "the institution of public penance" disappearing.[24] This disappearance in turn was due in part to the rise of private confessions on the part of the Irish monks who came into mainland Europe near the end of the sixth century under their leader St. Columban.

Because of this development of the eleventh century, another development took place in which "a violet veil was hung right across the church between the nave and sanctuary and thus for forty three days the altar."[25] The reason for this was that the faithful—now that it was no longer practical to dismiss all the sinners—did not feel that they as sinners were worthy to see the holy images of the cross and so forth until Holy Thursday. Over the centuries, this custom was later modified by having the statues and images covered only during Holy Week;[26] and after Vatican II it was allowed as an option for the episcopal conferences to decide.[27] In the last several years or so this practice has reemerged as an option.

With the appearance of the Missal of Pius V in 1570, the practice of distributing ashes among the faithful was located "before the celebration of the Eucharist. However, the name Ash Wednesday (Feria

---

22. *The Church at Prayer,* vol. 4: 67.

23. "The Liturgical Year," 185.

24. "The Liturgical Year," 185.

25. *Saint Andrew Daily Missal,* 196–97. See also *Reform,* 106.

26. *Saint Andrew Daily Missal,* 196–97. See also *Reform,* 106.

27. *Reform,* 106.

IV Cinerum) does not appear in the Roman Missal prior to the second half of the sixteenth century."[28]

Before Vatican II, Lent was divided into two parts. The first part is from Ash Wednesday until Saturday before Passion Sunday; and the second part is the two week period from Passion Sunday to Good Friday.[29] After Vatican II, this two week period (know as the Passiontide) was reduced from two weeks to one. Otherwise, as before Vatican II, it has two parts, but now the second part begins on Passion Sunday or Palm Sunday.

After Vatican II, the Sundays of Septuagesima, Sexagesima, and Quinquagesima Sundays were dropped; and the two weeks dedicated to the Passion of the Lord was reduced to one. Also, the days of fasting were limited to two: Ash Wednesday and Good Friday; and the days of abstinence were limited to Fridays. Another reform that took place was that of extending the focus from fasting to that of almsgiving and prayer. Before the Second Vatican Council the focus was strictly on that of fasting, or "giving up something". Now, while keeping the fast, two other focuses are added, prayer and almsgiving, just as it was before the sixth century.[30] It is interesting to note, that in the collects of the Missal of Paul VI there is one use of the word *eleemosyna* (for almsgiving) for this season but not the Missal of Pius V for the same season. The return to remembering prayer and almsgiving is a rediscovery of what Romano Gaurdini called a return to "a forgotten way of doing things and recapture lost attitudes."[31]

REV. GEORGE MANGIARACINA, O.C.D.

---

28. "The Liturgical Year," 185.

29. *Saint Andrew Daily Missal,* 196.

30. See also *Reform,* 92–94.

31. From "A Letter from Romano Guardini on the Essence of the Liturgical Act– 1964," available at the Web site of The National Institute for the Renewal of the Priesthood, Washington Theological Union, 6896 Laurel Street NW, Washington, DC, http://www.jknirp.com/guardf.htm.

PRAYER,
SCRIPTURE, AND
LECTIO DIVINA

Over the centuries, the faithful have developed many forms of prayer and meditation as a means of seeking communion with God. Meditation is a systematic way of putting oneself in God's presence in order to pray. Remember not to get lost in focusing on the steps of meditation, rather focus on the direct experience of encountering God.

VOCAL PRAYER

Along with meditation, we communicate with God through vocal prayer. This usually involves praying the Our Father, the Divine Office, or even the Mass. St. Teresa of Jesus said that those who pray with love and attention can, by the grace of God, be led to a contemplative state of union with him.[1]

---

1. See *Way of Perfection*, ch. 25.

MEDITATION

Meditation is a systematic way of arriving at union with God. It can involve picking up a book and reading over it until a passage appeals to you. You stop over it and think it over and, when you are ready, take that passage and make it the basis of your conversation with God.

A second approach is to make use of a meditation book with points of reflection prepared in advance. You go over each point one at a time until you are ready to enter into a conversation with God.

A third approach is to imagine Christ with you, or before you (for example, before taking the Blessed Sacrament) and speaking to him as one friend to another.

There are many more meditations, but the important thing is not to let them become ends in themselves, but a means to preparing yourself to be in God's presence and to be present to him when he discloses his presence to you. Some people experience, this presence as peace, or joy, or love. However, it is experienced, it should not be resisted. St. Teresa gives the example of someone who has a picture of a loved one, but after the loved one arrives the picture is let go of. The same is true with having a picture or practice of being in God's presence. Once God makes his presence felt, he or she does not hang onto the picture or practice but rather becomes present to God.

CONTEMPLATION

In the past, contemplation was considered to be a rare experience reserved for the saints. Not until around the end of the nineteenth century was contemplation understood to be the normal outgrowth of a life of Christian prayer.

While much has been written about contemplation, basically, contemplation is the sense of the quiet presence of God when in a state of prayer. That this is not so rare an event can be seen from the following story. Once upon a time, the Curé d'Ars saw a farmer quietly praying in church. One day he asked this farmer what was his prayer like; and the farmer said that sometimes he nods at me and sometimes I nod at him. In the words of John of the Cross,

"This is achieved in the state of union when the soul, in which God alone dwells, has no other function than that of an altar on which God is adored in praise and love" (Collected Works, 129).

LECTIO DIVINA

Lectio divina is a method of prayer that has lately been rediscovered. This is because it can be used with any spiritual text; and it consists of four easy steps: reading a text, mulling over it, praying from it, and being before God in quiet praise or presence.

For example, for the first Gospel reading of Lent for Ash Wednesday: Matthew 6:1–6, 16–18; the first step is to read it to make sense of it. You may find it helpful to have a Bible with you to check the footnotes to clear up any difficulty you have with the passage, or even consult a short Bible commentary.

The second step is to re-read the Gospel, pausing over those verses and words that strike you as meaningful—as though the Lord were speaking to you. Stay with these as long as they are meaningful for you. It is not expected that every verse or words in the whole Gospel will have the same attraction for you.

The third step flows from the second: you are now ready to speak to God in your own words on the basis of those verses or words that most impressed you. You may, as it were, compose your own prayer based on what you experienced in step two.

The fourth and final step is simply to rest in God's presence either praising him or just simply being present to him.

While all the steps are necessary in the beginning, as you pray, you may find yourself skipping step one and delving into step two; or perhaps skipping all the steps and being in God's presence with step four. In order not to let this become one more meditation, you should use this method only as it suits you. Once you encounter God, there is no longer any need for method.

DISTRACTIONS

One concern for many beginners in prayer is distractions. We try hard to fight them, but they will not go away. A better approach is to make them a part of prayer.

For example, suppose you have begun your period of prayer and you remember someone is sick in your family. You had not begun the period of prayer with the intention of thinking about this, but there it is. Instead of trying to suppress it, why not just talk to the Lord about it, trusting in his love and understanding? In time, this distraction, and others like it will fall by the wayside when the Lord communicates to you his love, peace, and joy.

REV. GEORGE MANGIARACINA, O.C.D.

ST. JOHN
OF THE CROSS:
ON FOLLOWING
JESUS CHRIST

Because John of the Cross is uncompromising and radical in his pursuit of God, he is difficult to read and follow. Yet if God is your goal then God must be your means to reach God. That is, because God is beyond all that he has created, there are no easy means to God. Since the theological virtues of faith, hope, and charity are the closest we can get to being of God, they are the closest means to God. Other means to God like images, devotions, religious experiences, and so forth are useful but they are, at best, remote means. As John of the Cross says,

"Consequently, a person who wants to arrive at union with the Supreme Repose and Good in this life must climb all the steps, which are considerations, forms, and concepts, and leave them behind, since they are dissimilar and unproportioned to the goal toward which they lead. And this goal is God. Accordingly, St. Paul teaches in the Acts of the Apostles: (translation from the original in Latin: We should not consider or esteem the

divinity to be like gold or silver, or stone sculptured by the artist, or like anything a person can fashion with the imagination [Acts 17:29])" (*Collected Works*, 187).

John of the Cross admits that his teaching is difficult, he says so in his prologue. He also laments that this true spirituality of following Christ on the Cross is so hard that he doubts that anyone can make it more attractive. As he says,

"Oh, who can make this counsel of our Savior on self-denial understandable, and practicable, and attractive, that spiritual persons might become aware of the difference between the method many of them think is good and the one that ought to be used in traveling this road! They are of the opinion that any kind of withdrawal from the world, or reformation of life, suffices. Some are content with a certain degree of virtue, perseverance in prayer, and mortification, but never achieve the nakedness, poverty, selflessness, or spiritual purity (which are all the same) about which the Lord counsels us here. For they still feed and clothe their natural selves with spiritual feelings and consolations instead of divesting and denying themselves of these for God's sake. They think denial of self in worldly matters is sufficient without annihilation and purification in the spiritual domain. It happens that, when some of this solid, perfect food (the annihilation of all sweetness in God—the pure spiritual cross and nakedness of Christ's poverty of spirit) is offered them in dryness, distaste, and trial, they run from it as from death and wander about in search only of sweetness and delightful communications from God. Such an attitude is not the hallmark of self-denial and nakedness of spirit but the indication of a spiritual sweet tooth. Through this kind of conduct they become, spiritually speaking, enemies of the cross of Christ [Phil 3:18]" (*Collected Works*, 170).

While I cannot make his teaching more *attractive*, I do believe that I can offer a way of understanding John of the Cross that will make this Lenten guide more fruitful. I propose to do this by showing that John of the Cross, in his writings, is basically answering three broad questions. Once you see these three broad questions and his answers to them, then you will understand why he proposed a challenging vision of following Christ as he did.

1. What is God's plan for the human race?
2. How are human beings to participate in this plan?
3. What is the result of participating in this plan?

The first question: What is God's plan for the human race?

For John of the Cross, God's plan for the human race is that each human being be united with him in an intimate and loving relationship. John of the Cross develops this view in his poems called the Romances.

"My Son, I wish to give you
a bride who will love you.
Because of you she will deserve
to share our company,
and eat at our table,
the same bread I eat,
that she may know the good
I have in such a Son;
and rejoice with me
in your grace and fullness."
"I am very grateful,"
the Son answered;
"I will show my brightness
to the bride you give me,
so that by it she may see
how great my Father is,
and how I have received
my being from your being.
I will hold her in my arms

and she will burn with your love,
and with eternal delight
she will exalt your goodness."

As God, the Father says:

Because of you she will deserve
to share our company,
and eat at our table,
the same bread I eat,
that she may know the good
I have in such a Son;
and rejoice with me
in your grace and fullness." ("On Creation," *Collected Works,* 62–64)

Thus, God the Father desired to create the human race so that it could share in God's company, eat at its table, know his Son, and rejoice with the Father in the grace and fullness of the Son. The Son in turn responded to the Father and said,

"I will show my brightness
to the bride you give me,
so that by it she may see
how great my Father is,
and how I have received
my being from your being.
I will hold her in my arms
and she will burn with your love,
and with eternal delight
she will exalt your goodness."

The Son, in responding to the Father, promised to show his brightness to the human race, his bride, so that they in turn may see how great God the Father is, how he, the Son received his being from the Father's being;

and how the Son in turn will so hold his new bride, the human race, that she will burn with the same love that burns in the Father's love and with eternal delight the human race will exult in the Father's goodness.

As a result, the whole goal of creation is that human beings be created out of the love that exists between the Father and the Son and for their participation in that same love. This is the foundation for his answer to the next two questions.

The second question: How are human beings to participate in this plan?

For John of the Cross, human beings are called to participate in this plan by a duel effort of making acts of self-denial and becoming motivated to do so when they are blessed with God's grace-filled presence. Just which one comes first (the movement of God towards the soul or the movement of the soul towards God), he does not say. Clearly, acts of self-denial of sensual and intellectual pleasures come from having been blessed by God's grace-filled presence; but it would be a mistake to wait around for this grace and do nothing until then. For the pre-experience of God's grace-filled presence, John of the Cross assumes that one is practicing prayer, growing in devotion, refusing to commit mortal sin, working against committing venial sins and so forth. He does not elaborate too much about this period. When he writes about beginners, he is presuming preparatory work in meditation, spiritual reading, and seeing a spiritual director. In the periods before and after grace-filled presence, one must make a concerted effort to let go of finding gratification in anything but God. John of the Cross' first two books in the Ascent of Mount Carmel are devoted to this end. His third book in the Ascent of Mount Carmel is devoted to what to do during the period of blessing by God's grace-filled presence.

The third question: What is the result of participating in this plan?

The short answer to the question: participation in the divine nature of God. In fact, it is why God created human beings, to participate in the divine nature of God. This is what John of the Cross understands Jesus to be saying to his Father in his priestly prayer when he speaks about eternal life as knowing the Father and Christ whom he sent. For John of the Cross, this is true living and true fulfillment. Every other kind of fulfillment is a bad counterfeit no matter how attractive it may seem.

Thus, the operative view of John of the Cross is this: God created human beings with his beauty, which became disfigured or wounded by sin. God originally created human beings beautiful so that they could participate in his divine life and would have sent his Son to culminate this work had human beings not sin. Though sin undid that plan, God continued to plan for the coming of his Son, no longer just as Spouse, but as Savior-Spouse to bring to completion his work of beautifying human beings so that we in turn could partake in his divine nature. This cost the Son of God his life on the Cross, but it would also show the way to true union with the Father.

As human beings with freedom, we can opt to partake in this plan by imitating Jesus Christ who is the way, the truth and the life or not. If we do so, it will cost us much in the way of denying ourselves the pleasures of the world. John of the Cross does not say we will never experience the pleasures that the world has to offer, but rather we will not seek them as ends in themselves since only God is an end in himself. Even the means to union with God are simply means. They should not be idolized.

Along with the means, we should also not place much stock in the experiences we receive from seeking God alone. Whether these experiences be consolation, peace, enjoyment, locutions, visions or visions about the future, these are all by-products of the union with God. To rest in these is again to keep ourselves from union with God.

What Jesus Christ Achieved with his Crucifixion

Since the whole point of the Lenten Season is to prepare ourselves to celebrate the Paschal mystery, I will touch upon John of the Cross' understanding of what Jesus Christ achieved by his crucifixion.

"Second, at the moment of his death he was certainly annihilated in his soul, without any consolation or relief, since the Father had left him that way in innermost aridity in the lower part. He was thereby compelled to cry out: My God, My God, why have you forsaken me? *[Mt 27:46].* *This was the most extreme abandonment, sensitively, that he had suffered in his life. And by it he accomplished the most marvelous work of his whole life, surpassing all the works and deeds and miracles that he had ever performed on earth or in heaven. That is, he brought about the reconciliation and union of the human race with God through grace"* (*Collected Works,* 172).

For John of the Cross, the primary effect of Jesus' death on the cross was that of reconciliation and union of the human race with God through grace. Most folks focus on the reconciliation aspect of Jesus' death of the cross, whereas John of the Cross includes the union of the human race with God through grace. God created the human race so that it and its members could live in the union of love that exists between the Father and the Son.

John of the Cross elaborates on this second aspect of *"union of the human race with God through grace"* in his Spiritual Canticle (B) where he says,

"For human nature, your mother, was corrupted in your first parents under the tree, and you too under the tree of the cross were restored. If your mother, therefore, brought you death under the tree, I brought you life under the tree of the cross. In such a way God manifests the decrees of his wisdom; he knows how to draw good from evil so wisely and beautifully, and to ordain to a greater good what was a cause of evil" (*Collected Works,* 564).

The Bridegroom himself literally speaks this stanza to the bride in the Song of Songs: *Sub arbore malo suscitavi te; ibi corrupta est mater tua, ibi violata est genitrix tua (Under the apple tree I raised you up; there your mother was corrupted, there she who bore you was violated)* [Sg 8:5].

"The espousal made on the cross is not the one we now speak of. For that espousal is accomplished immediately when God gives the first grace that is bestowed on each one at baptism. The espousal of which we speak bears reference to perfection and is not achieved save gradually and by stages. For though it is all one espousal, there is a difference in that one is attained at the soul's pace, and thus little by little, and the other at God's pace, and thus immediately" (Collected Works, 564).

In the Spiritual Canticle, John of the Cross sees the crucifixion of Jesus as a means of bringing the life lost by original sin back to the human race. That this restoration was not merely a bringing back of the previous lost state, John of the Cross says there was an espousal on the Cross between the human race and God. This espousalship becomes available to everyone at baptism; but it still needs to be integrated in stages. From these two texts, we can see that for John of the Cross, the crucifixion of Jesus brought reconciliation with God, restoration, and union through grace in the form of an espousal between God and the human race.

It is because it cost Jesus Christ so much, John of the Cross says Christians must undergo the same. Implicit in this was his awareness of what St. Paul said that as we share much in the sufferings of Christ so too shall we share in the consolation and the glory (2 Cor 1:3–7 NAB 1970); and be enabled, as St. Peter said, to become partakers of the divine nature sharing in the same love that the Father and the Son have for each other (2 Pt 1–3).

In other words, if you were to ask John of the Cross what life was all about, he would respond, sharing in the same self-emptying love that the Father and the Son have for one another.

REV. GEORGE MANGIARACINA, O.C.D.

ON
THE DAILY
SCRIPTURES

As noted, this book presents daily readings and prayers for every day of Lent, weekdays, and Sundays. The daily readings begin with a Gospel Reading, followed by a quote from St. John of the Cross' writings, a reflection, and a prayer.

The daily Gospel Reading is from the Roman Catholic *Lectionary for Mass for Use in the Dioceses of the United States of America*. The *Lectionary for Mass* contains the readings for Mass selected from the Bible.

If you were to attend daily Mass during Lent in the United States, you would hear the same daily Gospel Readings included in this book. For example, the Ash Wednesday Gospel Reading, Matthew 6:1–6, 16–18, is the same Gospel Reading you would hear when you attend Mass to receive your ashes. In fact, on each day at all the Masses of the Latin-rite Roman Catholic Church throughout the world, you will hear the same readings at Mass, read in the vernacular language or Latin.

There are two main components of the Lectionary: Sunday and Weekday readings. Sunday readings are arranged on a three-year cycle: Year A, Year B, and Year C. The Gospel readings for Year A are generally from the Gospel of St. Matthew, Year B are generally from the Gospel of St. Mark and Year C are generally from Gospel of St. Luke. St. John's Gospel is read on Sundays in Year A, B, and C during specific liturgical calendar periods.

The Weekday readings are on a two-year cycle: Year I and Year II. Year I are odd-numbered years and Year II are even- numbered years. However, the weekday readings during Lent are the same for Year I and Year II but differ each day. In this book, the weekday Gospel Readings are also the weekday Gospel Readings in the Lectionary.

For Sundays in this book, you have three different selections of readings and prayers. Each selection begins with a different Gospel Reading, the Gospel Reading from Year A, B, or C of the Lectionary.

Appendix A, the Calendar for Lent 2010–2019 & Lectionary Cycle, lists the specific dates for the next ten years for Ash Wednesday, the Sundays of Lent, and includes the Sunday Lectionary Cycle for the year. Please refer to the table to determine the current year's Sunday Lectionary Cycle: Year A, B, or C and select the appropriate Sunday Gospel Reading for the present year.

This book in a small way invites you to pray each day with the Church and your fellow Christians in the world on your Lenten Journey with Jesus Christ and St. John of the Cross.

PETER J. MONGEAU

"Well and good if all things change, Lord God, provided we are rooted in you" (Sayings of Light and Love 1.34).

ST. JOHN OF THE CROSS

ASH
WEDNESDAY
*and the Days
after Ash Wednesday*

GOSPEL

JESUS SAID TO HIS DISCIPLES:

"Take care not to perform righteous deeds in order that people may see them; otherwise, you will have no recompense from your heavenly Father. When you give alms, do not blow a trumpet before you, as the hypocrites do in the synagogues and in the streets to win the praise of others. Amen, I say to you, they have received their reward. But when you give alms, do not let your left hand know what your right is doing, so that your almsgiving may be secret. And your Father who sees in secret will repay you.

"When you pray, do not be like the hypocrites, who love to stand and pray in the synagogues and on street corners so that others may see them. Amen, I say to you, they have received their reward. But when you pray, go to your inner room, close the door, and pray to your Father in secret. And your Father who sees in secret will repay you.

"When you fast, do not look gloomy like the hypocrites. They neglect their appearance, so that they may appear to others to be fasting. Amen, I say to you, they have received their reward. But when you fast, anoint your head and wash your face, so that you may not appear to be fasting, except to your Father who is hidden. And your Father who sees what is hidden will repay you."

MATTHEW 6: 1-6, 16-18

ST. JOHN OF THE CROSS

Here St. John of the Cross gives us the spiritual attitude for doing the works of Lent: prayer, fasting and giving alms.

"For the sake of directing their joy in moral goods to God, Christians should keep in mind that the value of their good works, fasts, alms, penances, and so on, is not based on quantity and quality so much as on the love of God practiced in them; and consequently that these works are of greater excellence in the measure both that the love of God by which they are performed is more pure and entire and that self-interest diminishes with respect to pleasure, comfort, praise, and earthly or heavenly joy. They should not set their heart on the pleasure, comfort, savor, and other elements of self-interest these good works and practices usually entail, but recollect their joy in God and desire to serve him through these means. And through purgation and darkness as to this joy in moral goods they should desire in secret that only God be pleased and joyful over their works. They should have no other interest or satisfaction than the honor and glory of God. Thus all the strength of their will in regard to these moral goods will be recollected in God" (A 3.27.5).

REFLECTION

Ash Wednesday is a sober beginning for the Season of Lent. The readings, the ashes, and the whole tenor of the Mass signal that something grave has begun. On it hangs our identity as Christians and whether or not we will express in our behavior what we believe in our hearts. In the readings, both Jesus and John of the Cross point to the importance of the heart in this season. Both caution us against becoming complacent with a mere performance of practices; both urge us to look within and see where in our lives we have taken message of Christ seriously; and where we may have not taken his message seriously. While the season has a somber start, its aim is to have a joyful end in our Lord's Resurrection. So let us begin, and get to work.

PRAYER

Lord, you have called us to follow you during this Season of Lent through prayer, fasting, and almsgiving. Grant, we ask, that as we follow you through these practices, we may do them for love of you alone and so prepare ourselves to share in your self-emptying on the Cross, which you did for love of your Father alone. We ask this in your name, Amen.

GOSPEL

JESUS SAID TO HIS DISCIPLES:

"The Son of Man must suffer greatly and be rejected by the elders, the chief priests, and the scribes, and be killed and on the third day be raised."

Then he said to all, "If anyone wishes to come after me, he must deny himself and take up his cross daily and follow me. For whoever wishes to save his life will lose it, but whoever loses his life for my sake will save it. What profit is there for one to gain the whole world yet lose or forfeit himself?"

LUKE 9: 22-25

ST. JOHN OF THE CROSS

St John of the Cross comments on this passage that is cited in both Matthew and Mark.

"A genuine spirit seeks rather the distasteful in God than the delectable, leans more toward suffering than toward consolation, more toward going without everything for God than toward possession, and toward dryness and affliction than toward sweet consolation. It knows that this is the significance of following Christ and denying self, that the other method is perhaps a seeking of self in God—something entirely contrary to love. Seeking oneself in God is the same as looking for the caresses and consolations of God. Seeking God in oneself entails not only the desire to do without these consolations for God's sake, but also the inclination to choose for love of Christ all that is most distasteful whether in God or in the world; and this is what loving God means" (A 2.7.5b).

REFLECTION

If yesterday's start was somber, today's Gospel is no less so as Jesus speaks of the suffering and death that are to come in his life. With this Gospel, he is already anticipating what we will be celebrating during Holy Week when we follow him through his Passion. St. John of the Cross gives us the attitude we should have in following Jesus: have an orientation to what is more difficult than what is easier; go by the path of most resistance rather than the least. He believes that if we do this, then we will be closer to putting the Gospel in practice than not. We will be more on target than off target. The final goal for John of the Cross is not that we go about feeling like miserable human beings; but rather be united with God in the depths of our being.

PRAYER

Lord, God, you call us to follow your Son in imitation of his example by denying our very self, and taking up our cross daily. Grant, we ask, that we may do so by persevering in our commitments for Lent and thus arrive as the sons and daughters of your Kingdom. We ask this through Christ, our Lord, Amen.

GOSPEL

The disciples of John approached Jesus and said, "Why do we and the Pharisees fast much, but your disciples do not fast?" Jesus answered them, "Can the wedding guests mourn as long as the bridegroom is with them? The days will come when the bridegroom is taken away from them, and then they will fast."

MATTHEW 9: 14-15

ST. JOHN OF THE CROSS

In this Gospel account, Jesus tells his disciples there cannot be union between two different things: His presence and the disciples' mourning. St. John of the Cross teaches, two contrary things cannot abide in the same person, for example, the joy of Christ's presence and doing things for one's own satisfaction.

"No creature, none of its actions and abilities, can reach or encompass God's nature. Consequently, a soul must strip itself of everything pertaining to creatures and of its actions and abilities (of its understanding, satisfaction, and feeling), so that when everything unlike and unconformed to God is cast out, it may receive the likeness of God. And the soul will receive this likeness because nothing contrary to the will of God will be left in it. Thus it will be transformed in God" (A 2.5.4b).

REFLECTION

We live in a world where we can have our cake and eat it too. We find every inconvenience a nuisance and every difficulty an obstacle to be removed. Both Jesus and John of the Cross know that this attitude blinds us to the true state of affairs. Jesus knows that you cannot fast when you are happy; and John of the Cross knows that no created person, place, or thing is equal to God. They may for a time serve the purpose of finding God, once God is found, we must detach from that person, place, or thing. May their teaching on the incompatibility of having our desires for people, places, and things, and having them apart from God, lead us to see the truth with new eyes during the Season of Lent.

PRAYER

Lord, God, you call us through the Season of Lent to undergo a change of heart through fasting. Grant, we ask, that as we work with you to free ourselves of all that is contrary to the Spirit of your Son, we may be ready to receive the new wine of the Holy Spirit in new wineskins when he comes upon us at Pentecost. We asked this through Christ, your Son, Amen.

GOSPEL

Jesus saw a tax collector named Levi sitting at the customs post. He said to him, "Follow me." And leaving everything behind, he got up and followed him. Then Levi gave a great banquet for him in his house, and a large crowd of tax collectors and others were at table with them. The Pharisees and their scribes complained to his disciples, saying, "Why do you eat and drink with tax collectors and sinners?" Jesus said to them in reply, "Those who are healthy do not need a physician, but the sick do. I have not come to call the righteous to repentance but sinners."

LUKE 5: 27-32

ST. JOHN OF THE CROSS

Here St. John of the Cross speaks of another sinner who lets go of her sinful ways, Mary Magdalene.

"Mary Magdalene, in spite of her past, paid no heed to the crowds of people, prominent as well as unknown, at the banquet. She did not consider the propriety of weeping and shedding tears in the presence of our Lord's guests. Her only concern was to reach him for whom her soul was already wounded and on fire, without any delay and without waiting for another more appropriate time [Lk 7:37–38]. And such is the inebriation and courage of love: Knowing that her Beloved was shut up in the tomb by a huge sealed rock and surrounded by guards so the disciples could not steal his body, she did not permit this to keep her from going out with ointments before daybreak to anoint him [Mt 27:64–66; Mk 16:1–2; Jn. 20:1]"(N 2.13.6).

REFLECTION

The foundation of all spiritual growth is self-knowledge. Levi, who became Matthew, saw his sinfulness in the light of Jesus' love for him and underwent a change of heart to become his disciple. Mary Magdalene also saw her sinfulness in the light of Jesus' love for her and likewise underwent a change of heart to become Jesus' disciple. To see our true state as sinners in the light of God's love is disconcerting at first; but when acknowledged and accepted it leads to the freedom to undergo all sufferings for the sake of the one who sets us free.

PRAYER

Lord God, through this Season of Lent you call us to a deeper life of faith and union with you through Christ, your Son. Grant, we ask, that no attachments to our past (whether innocent or sinful) keep us from dining with the Risen Lord at Easter. We ask this through Christ, our Lord, Amen.

FIRST WEEK
OF
LENT

GOSPEL

At that time Jesus was led by the Spirit into the desert to be tempted by the devil. He fasted for forty days and forty nights, and afterwards he was hungry. The tempter approached and said to him, "If you are the Son of God, command that these stones become loaves of bread."

He said in reply, "It is written: / *One does not live on bread alone, / but on every word that comes forth from the mouth of God."* / Then the devil took him to the holy city, and made him stand on the parapet of the temple, and said to him, "If you are the Son of God, throw yourself down. For it is written: / *He will command his angels concerning you / and with their hands they will support you, / lest you dash your foot against a stone."* / Jesus answered him, "Again it is written, *You shall not put the Lord, your God, to the test."* Then the devil took him up to a very high mountain, and showed him all the kingdoms of the world in their magnificence, and he said to him, "All these I shall give to you, if you will prostrate yourself and worship me." At this, Jesus said to him, "Get away, Satan! It is written: / *The Lord, your God, shall you worship / and him alone shall you serve."* / Then the devil left him and, behold, angels came and ministered to him.

MATTHEW 4: 1-11

ST. JOHN OF THE CROSS

John of the Cross speaks about curtailing our inordinate desires for people, places, or things. He calls inordinate desires "appetites."

"Oh, if spiritual persons knew how much spiritual good and abundance they lose by not attempting to raise their appetites above childish things, and if they knew to what extent, by not desiring the taste of these trifles, they would discover in this simple spiritual food the savor of all things! The Israelites did not perceive the taste of every other food that was contained in the manna, because their appetite was not centered on this manna alone. They were unsuccessful in deriving from the manna all the taste and strength they were looking for, not because the manna didn't have these but because of their craving for other foods. Similarly, those who love something together with God undoubtedly make little of God, for they weigh in the balance with God an object far distant from God, as we have said.

"It is well known from experience that when the will is attached to an object, it esteems that object higher than any other, even though another, not as pleasing, may deserve higher admiration. And if people desire pleasure from two objects, they are necessarily offensive to the more deserving because through their desire for both they equate the two. Since nothing equals God, those who love and are attached to something along with God offend him exceedingly. If this is true, what would happen if they loved something more than God?" (A 1.5.4–5).

REFLECTION

The Season of Lent challenges us to take up prayer, fasting, and almsgiving as part of our following Christ in preparation for Good Friday and Easter. This First Sunday of Lent begins with Jesus fasting in the desert for forty days and nights, after which he was hungry.

For John of the Cross there is a hunger that underlies all hungers that can be satisfied by God alone. However, because God is hidden and cannot be experienced as he is, we direct that hunger to be fulfilled in people, places, things, or food. John of the Cross knows that we have a legitimate need for these but he wishes to lead us away from substituting them for God.

If we were able to have a reasonable desire for people, places, things, or food, we would not be mistaking them for God. As it is, we are corrupted by original sin and so we become unreasonable in our desire for these. What John of the Cross directs us to do, in a sense, is to fast from our desires for these, and to find our fulfillment in God alone. When we do, we then have a reasonable desire for them and so there is no conflict in the priority we have for God and our receiving what we need from God. This is what Jesus meant when he said: *One does not live on bread alone but on every word that comes from the mouth of God.* John of the Cross, you might say, wants us to direct the mouth of our desires (or appetites) to the Words of God's love alone so that we may experience what our Lord taught the tempter in the desert.

PRAYER

Lord, God, you have invited us to know you through fasting and prayer in imitation of your Son. Grant, we ask, the grace to overcome our hungers for all that is not you, and by the strength of your Holy Spirit direct them to you alone. We ask this through Christ, your Son, Amen.

GOSPEL

The Spirit drove Jesus out into the desert, and he remained in the desert for forty days, tempted by Satan. He was among wild beasts, and the angels ministered to him.

After John had been arrested, Jesus came to Galilee proclaiming the gospel of God: "This the time of fulfillment. The kingdom of God is at hand. Repent, and believe in the gospel."

MARK 1: 12-15

ST. JOHN OF THE CROSS

Here St. John of the Cross speaks of those who have been to the desert.

"Those whom God begins to lead into these desert solitudes are like the children of Israel. When God began giving them the heavenly food, which contained in itself all savors and changed to whatever taste each one hungered after [Wis 16:20–21], as is there mentioned, they nonetheless felt a craving for the tastes of the fleshmeats and onions they had eaten in Egypt, for their palate was accustomed and attracted to them more than to the delicate sweetness of the angelic manna. And in the midst of that heavenly food, they wept and sighed for fleshmeat [Nm 11:4–6]. The baseness of our appetite is such that it makes us long for our own miserable goods and feel aversion for the incommunicable heavenly good.

"Yet, as I say, when these aridities are the outcome of the purgative way of the sensory appetite, the spirit feels the strength and energy to work, which is obtained from the substance of that interior food, even though in the beginning it may not experience the savor, for the reason just mentioned. This food is the beginning of a contemplation that is dark and dry to the senses. Ordinarily this contemplation, which is secret and hidden from the very one who receives it, imparts to the soul, together with the dryness and emptiness it produces in the senses, an inclination to remain alone and in quietude. And the soul will be unable to dwell on any particular thought, nor will it have the desire to do so" (N 1.9.5–6).

REFLECTION

Probably, there is no more disconcerting experience than to be thrust into a crisis. For some people this involves losing their health and being in danger of death. For others it involves losing their job and being unemployed. For others it involves losing a friend, a spouse, or someone very important. All of these, for some people, make up a desert experience where they find themselves with few resources and a great need to rely on God. Mark's Gospel presents Jesus as being thrust into the desert by the Holy Spirit. He does not elaborate on the temptations Jesus underwent but, rather, focuses on his being thrust there by the Spirit, the conflict with the tempter, and his being waited upon by the angels to highlight his being Lord.

John of the Cross describes a similar experience of being thrust into the desert which he calls the dark night. Sometimes, it is provoked by the experiences I alluded to earlier but it brings with it much more. It is a time when God reorders our desires for people, places, and things to himself alone. This is a very disconcerting experience since there is very little to go on except that whereas before we found satisfaction in them, now we do not. As John of the Cross says: *And the soul will be unable to dwell on any particular thought, nor will it have the desire to do so.* Thus, whereas before we could direct our hunger to them, now we cannot. It is, in a sense, God becoming the Lord of what we desire to desiring all through him.

PRAYER

Lord, God, you have called us into the discipline of Lent as your Spirit led your Son into the desert. Grant, we ask, that we may embrace the dryness of fulfilling our Lenten resolutions, so that we may enjoy even now, the joy the Holy Spirit's presence. We ask this through Christ, our Lord, Amen.

GOSPEL

Filled with the Holy Spirit, Jesus returned from the Jordan and was led by the Spirit into the desert for forty days, to be tempted by the devil. He ate nothing during those days, and when they were over he was hungry. The devil said to him, "If you are the Son of God, command this stone to become bread." Jesus answered him, "It is written, *One does not live on bread alone.*" Then he took him up and showed him all the kingdoms of the world in a single instant. The devil said to him, "I shall give to you all this power and glory; for it has been handed over to me, and I may give it to whomever I wish. All this will be yours, if you worship me." Jesus said to him in reply, "It is written: / *You shall worship the Lord, your God, and him alone shall you serve.*" / Then he led them to Jerusalem, made him stand on the parapet of the temple, and said to him, "If you are the Son of God, throw yourself down from here, for it is written: / *He will command his angels concerning you, to guard you,* / and: / *With their hands they will support you,* / *lest you dash your foot against a stone.*" / Jesus said to him in reply, "It also says, *You shall not put the Lord, your God, to the test.*" When the devil had finished every temptation, he departed from him for a time.

LUKE 4: 1-13

ST. JOHN OF THE CROSS

St. John of the Cross deals with the harm that occurs to those who succumb to temptation. Here he speaks the harm that comes from finding joy in performing acts of prophecy.

"Through these passages we learn that the harm engendered by this joy comes not only from the wicked and perverse use of God's graces—as in the case of Balaam and those who deceived the people with their miracles—but even from performing them without God's grace, as in those who prophesied their fancies and spoke of visions manufactured by either themselves or the devil. When the devil observes their attachment to these wonders, he opens a wide field, provides ample material for their endeavors, and meddles extensively. And these individuals with such means spread wide their sails, become shamelessly audacious, and abound in prodigious works.

"And this is not all! The joy and covetousness they have in these works reaches such a point that if previously their pact with the devil was secret—for often the works are performed through a secret pact—now through their boldness they make an express and open one with him and by an agreement subject themselves to him as his disciples and friends. Hence we have wizards, enchanters, magicians, soothsayers, and witches.

"Joy in these works goes so far that some, as Simon Magus, not merely want to buy gifts and graces with money [Acts 8:18] for the service of the devil, but they even try to get hold of sacred and divine objects—which cannot be mentioned without trembling—as has already been witnessed in the theft of the most sacred body of our Lord Jesus Christ for evil practices and abominations. May God extend and show forth his infinite mercy in this matter!" (A 3.31.4–5).

REFLECTION

In the film, *The Lord of the Rings,* Boromir sees power of the ring and is tempted to use it to save his kingdom Gondor. The more he looked upon it, the more he desired to steal the ring from Frodo. This momentary loss of his guard kept him from seeing the Orcs preparing to attack the Fellowship and led to his death.

John of the Cross does not deny that there are wondrous powers in the spiritual world. His concern is that we make use of them to separate ourselves from God. In times like ours, like Boromir, we are tempted to wish we had more luck or some extra power to save ourselves or those we love. Neither Jesus, nor John of the Cross teach us this. As Jesus said: *You shall not put the Lord, your God, to the test.*

PRAYER

Lord God, you call us to follow your Son through the Season of Lent so that we may know the joy of the Holy Spirit. Grant, we ask, that we may take no joy in the use of the spiritual or material gifts you may have given us but in the knowledge of knowing that we have been called to be partakers of your divine nature through Christ your Son. We ask this through Christ, Our Lord. Amen.

GOSPEL

JESUS SAID TO HIS DISCIPLES:

"When the Son of Man comes in his glory, and all the angels with him, he will sit upon his glorious throne, and all the nations will be assembled before him. And he will separate them one from another, as a shepherd separates the sheep from the goats. He will place the sheep on his right and the goats on his left. Then the king will say to those on his right, 'Come, you who are blessed by my Father. Inherit the kingdom prepared for you from the foundation of the world. For I was hungry and you gave me food, I was thirsty and you gave me drink, a stranger and you welcomed me, naked and you clothed me, ill and you cared for me, in prison and you visited me.' Then the righteous will answer him and say, 'Lord, when did we see you hungry and feed you, or thirsty and give you drink? When did we see you a stranger and welcome you, or naked and clothe you? When did we see you ill or in prison, and visit you?' And the king will say to them in reply, 'Amen, I say to you, whatever you did for one of these least brothers of mine, you did for me.' Then he will say to those on his left, 'Depart from me, you accursed, into the eternal fire prepared for the Devil and his angels. For I was hungry and you gave me no food, I was thirsty and you gave me no drink, a stranger and you gave me no welcome, naked and you gave me no clothing, ill and in prison, and you did not care for me.' Then they will answer and say, 'Lord, when did we see you hungry or thirsty or a stranger or naked or ill or in prison, and not minister to your needs?' He will answer them, 'Amen, I say to you, what you did not do for one of these least ones, you did not do for me.' And these will go off to eternal punishment, but the righteous to eternal life."

MATTHEW 25: 31-46

ST. JOHN OF THE CROSS

Here St. John of the Cross focuses on the correct interior disposition for a work of charity.

"Speaking now of supernatural gifts and graces, as we here understand them, I assert that for the purgation of vain joy regarding them it is appropriate to note two benefits, temporal and spiritual, that are included in this kind of goods.

"The temporal includes healing the sick, restoring sight to the blind, raising the dead, expelling devils, prophesying the future so people may be careful, and other similar things. The spiritual and eternal benefit is the knowledge and love of God caused by these works either in those who perform them or in those in whom, or before whom, they are accomplished.

"As for the first, the temporal benefit, supernatural works and miracles merit little or no joy of soul. When the second benefit is excluded they are of little or no importance to human beings, since they are not in themselves a means for uniting the soul with God, as is charity. And the exercise of these supernatural works and graces does not require grace and charity; either God truly bestows them as he did to the wicked prophet Balaam [Nm 22:20] and to Solomon, or they are effected falsely by means of the devil, as in the case of Simon Magus [Acts 8:9–11], or by means of other secret, natural powers. If any of these marvels were to be beneficial to their agent, they were those that were true, given by God" (A 3.30.3–4).

REFLECTION

A characteristic of John of the Cross is to focus on our desires for food, clothing, shelter, glory, rest and so forth. For him, the real challenge of life is not doing more, or less, but the cultivation of doing, in a selfless manner, what the responsibilities in our state of life call us to do. So, for him, if a disciple were to feed the hungry, cloth the naked, and so forth, and did these for his own joy and satisfaction, he would derive no spiritual profit from them. He would have already received his own reward by looking for his own self-approval in them, rather than in the knowledge and love of God. In other words, those who draw attention to themselves for their own self-satisfaction, lose their reward from God.

PRAYER

O Lord, through this Season of Lent, you invite us to recall your blessings and share them with those in need. Grant, we ask, that we may attend to those in need with a true selfless disposition that imitates the manner in which you have blessed us. We ask this through Christ, our Lord. Amen.

GOSPEL

Jesus said to his disciples:

"In praying, do not babble like the pagans, who think that they will be heard because of their many words. Do not be like them. Your Father knows what you need before you ask him.

"This is how you are to pray:

Our Father who art in heaven,
    hallowed be thy name,
    thy Kingdom come,
thy will be done,
    on earth as it is in heaven.
Give us this day our daily bread;
and forgive us our trespasses,
    as we forgive those who trespass against us;
and lead us not into temptation,
    but deliver us from evil.

"If you forgive men their transgressions, your heavenly Father will forgive you. But if you do not forgive men, neither will your Father forgive your transgressions."

MATTHEW 6: 7-15

ST. JOHN OF THE CROSS

St. John of the Cross writes at great length about the attitude we should have when making an intercession before God.

"*The Lord has promised in the Gospel:* Seek first, and chiefly, the kingdom of God and his justice, and all these other things will be added unto you [Mt 6:33]. *This is the aim and petition that is most pleasing to God. To obtain an answer to the requests we bear in our hearts, there is no better means than to concentrate the strength of our prayers on what is more pleasing to God. Then he will give us not only the salvation we beg for but whatever else he sees is fit and good for us, even though we do not ask for it. David shows this clearly in a psalm:* The Lord is near to those who call on him in truth [Ps 145:18], *to those who ask for things that are most true, such as things pertinent to salvation. Of these individuals he says afterward:* He will fulfill the will of those who fear him, and he will hear their prayers and save them. For God is the guardian of those who love him [Ps 145:19–20]. *God's being near, of which David speaks, is nothing more than his satisfying them and granting what it did not even enter their minds to ask for. We read that because Solomon had asked for something pleasing to God (that is, wisdom) so as to be certain of ruling the people justly, God answered him:* Because wisdom pleased you more than any other thing, and you did not seek victory through the death of your enemies, or riches, or a long life, not only will I give you the wisdom you seek to rule my people justly, but I will even give you what you have not asked for, that is, riches and substance and glory so that no king, either before you or after you, will be like you [2 Chron 1:11–12]. *And God in fact did this and pacified Solomon's enemies, too, so that all who were around him paid him tribute and did not perturb him* [1 Kgs. 4:21–24]" (A 3.44.2).

REFLECTION

One of the earliest characteristics of Christians was their manner of prayer. This is not to say other folks did not pray; but rather that Christians approached prayer with an attitude of trusting God to answer their prayers through Christ. John of the Cross was a man of prayer and he taught his disciples that the best way to pray was to always seek what was more pleasing to God. To his way of thinking, the more we focus on what is pleasing to God, the less we are tied to having things work our according our pleasure. Another way of putting this is: the more we become selfless in our prayer, the more God-like we become; and that is the goal of all prayer in John of the Cross: become like God by participating in his divine nature.

PRAYER

God, our Father, your Son taught us how to pray with trust in you and in forgiving those who offend us. Grant, we ask, that we may grow in trust of your love for us, and in our ability to forgive as you have forgiven us, so that we may be witnesses of your Son's presence in the world. We ask this through Christ, our Lord. Amen.

GOSPEL

While still more people gathered in the crowd, Jesus said to them, "This generation is an evil generation; it seeks a sign, but no sign will be given it, except the sign of Jonah. Just as Jonah became a sign to the Ninevites, so will the Son of Man be to this generation. At the judgment the queen of the south will rise with the men of this generation and she will condemn them, because she came from the ends of the earth to hear the wisdom of Solomon, and there is something greater than Solomon here. At the judgment the men of Nineveh will arise with this generation and condemn it, because at the preaching of Jonah they repented, and there is something greater than Jonah here."

LUKE 11: 29-32

ST. JOHN OF THE CROSS

St. John of the Cross comments on how God responds to those who seek extraordinary visions and locutions.

"Those who now desire to question God or receive some vision or revelation are guilty not only of foolish behavior but also of offending him by not fixing their eyes entirely on Christ and by living with the desire for some other novelty.

"God could answer as follows: If I have already told you all things in my Word, my Son, and if I have no other word, what answer or revelation can I now make that would surpass this? Fasten your eyes on him alone because in him I have spoken and revealed all and in him you will discover even more than you ask for and desire. You are making an appeal for locutions and revelations that are incomplete, but if you turn your eyes to him you will find them complete. For he is my entire locution and

response, vision and revelation, which I have already spoken, answered, manifested, and revealed to you by giving him to you as a brother, companion, master, ransom, and reward. On that day when I descended on him with my Spirit on Mount Tabor proclaiming: . . . (This is my beloved Son in whom I am well pleased, hear him) [Mt 17:5], *I gave up these methods of answering and teaching and presented them to him. Hear him because I have no more faith to reveal or truths to manifest. If I spoke before, it was to promise Christ. If they questioned me, their inquiries were related to their petitions and longings for Christ in whom they were to obtain every good, as is now explained in all the doctrine of the evangelists and apostles. But now those who might ask me in that way and desire that I speak and reveal something to them would somehow be requesting Christ again and more faith, yet they would be failing in faith because it has already been given in Christ. Accordingly, they would offend my beloved Son deeply because they would not merely be failing him in faith, but obliging him to become incarnate and undergo his life and death again. You will not find anything to ask or desire of me through revelations and visions. Behold him well, for in him you will uncover all of these already made and given, and many more"* (A 2.22.5).

REFLECTION

Early in his ministry, Jesus cast a devil out of someone (Lk 10:14) and he was accused of having done so by the power of Beelzebub. It was in this context that many were seeking a sign from God to validate his ministry. Jesus told them, in a sense, that they would not see God validate his ministry until his Resurrection, just as Jonah was validated when his preaching was accepted by the Ninevites.

While we have two thousand years behind us as followers of Christ, there are still some who seek signs. Usually, they seek signs for the end times, or for messages from Mary about the future. For John of the Cross, all this is useless. God has already said all he needed to say in his Son. Why trouble him further? The Son of God is the message that has been validated for two thousand years.

PRAYER

Lord God, you have revealed all that we need to know for our salvation in the sacred scriptures, and especially in your Son. Grant, we ask, not to trouble you any more for special revelations but to trust instead in your abiding presence through your Son in the Holy Spirit. We ask this through Christ, your Son. Amen.

GOSPEL

JESUS SAID TO HIS DISCIPLES:

"Ask and it will be given to you; seek and you will find; knock and the door will be opened to you. For everyone who asks, receives; and the one who seeks, finds; and to the one who knocks, the door will be opened. Which one of you would hand his son a stone when he asked for a loaf of bread, or a snake when he asked for a fish? If you then, who are wicked, know how to give good gifts to your children, how much more will your heavenly Father give good things to those who ask him.

"Do to others whatever you would have them do to you. This is the law and the prophets."

MATTHEW 7: 7-12

ST. JOHN OF THE CROSS

St. John of the Cross had confidence in God answering his prayers, but he was more concerned with having faith in God's intentions in answering his prayers.

"It is impossible for someone unspiritual to judge and understand the things of God correctly; and one is not spiritual if one judges them according to the senses. And thus even though these things are clothed in what is of the senses, they are not understood. This is what St. Paul really asserts: . . . (The animal person fails to perceive the things that are of the spirit of God, for they are foolishness to him, and he is unable to understand them because they are spiritual. Yet the spiritual person judges all things) [1 Cor 2:14–15]. *'The animal person' refers to those who use only the senses; 'the spiritual person' to those who are neither bound to nor guided by the senses. It is therefore rash to dare communicate with God by means of supernatural, sensory apprehensions, or to allow anyone to do so.*

"For the sake of greater clarity here are some examples: Suppose God says to a saintly man who is deeply afflicted because of persecution by his enemies: 'I will free you from your enemies.' This prophecy could be true; nonetheless the man's enemies will prevail and kill him. Anyone who had given these words a temporal interpretation would have been deceived because God had been speaking of the true and principal freedom and victory—salvation, in which the soul is free and victorious over all its enemies much more truly and loftily than if liberated from them here below. This prophecy had greater truth and richness than was understandable through an interpretation that related the freedom to this life. By his words, God always refers to the more important and profitable meaning, whereas humans will refer the words to a less important sense, in their own way and for their own purpose, and thus be deceived" (A 2.19.11b–12).

REFLECTION

Jesus promised his disciples that those who ask in faith will receive. John of the Cross believes this too, but he is quick to caution that what God gives us may be beyond our understanding which is limited to our experience and way of perceiving. It takes time to develop a spiritual sense of how and when God answers our prayers. In other words, "the third day" we await may be more than three mere days. It may in fact be "the third day" of our eternal life in heaven.

PRAYER

Lord, God, your Son prayed to you with heartfelt trust at Gethsemane, and he put faith in your silence to accept your will. Grant, we ask, that we too may have this childlike trust in you as the sons and daughters he merited for you on the Cross. We ask this through Christ, your Son. Amen.

GOSPEL

JESUS SAID TO HIS DISCIPLES:

"I tell you, unless your righteousness surpasses that of the scribes and Pharisees, you will not enter into the Kingdom of heaven.

"You have heard that it was said to your ancestors, *You shall not kill; and whoever kills will be liable to judgment.* But I say to you, whoever is angry with his brother will be liable to judgment, and whoever says to his brother, *Raqa,* will be answerable to the Sanhedrin, and whoever says, 'You fool,' will be liable to fiery Gehenna. Therefore, if you bring your gift to the altar, and there recall that your brother has anything against you, leave your gift there at the altar, go first and be reconciled with your brother, and then come and offer your gift. Settle with your opponent quickly while on the way to court. Otherwise your opponent will hand you over to the judge, and the judge will hand you over to the guard, and you will be thrown into prison. Amen, I say to you, you will not be released until you have paid the last penny."

MATTHEW 5: 20-26

ST. JOHN OF THE CROSS

Here St. John of the Cross writes on the need for keeping things in perspective when dealing with difficult people and situations.

"Do not let what is happening to me, daughter, cause you any grief, for it does not cause me any. What greatly grieves me is that one who is not at fault is blamed. Men do not do these things, but God, who knows what is suitable for us and arranges things for our own good. Think nothing else but that God ordains all, and where there is no love, put love, and you will draw out love" (L 26; July 6, 1591).

REFLECTION

When John of the Cross wrote this letter he was being persecuted for standing up to Doria in his treatment of the nuns. What followed was that John of the Cross was relieved of all his responsibilities, in part because another friar was out to seek his removal from the order. John of the Cross does not retaliate by wishing harm on this friar. Rather, he fears that this friar will be blamed when John can clearly see that it is God at work through him. Thus, John of the Cross does not call the friar names or wish judgment on him. Instead, he strives to let his love grow in the light of the Gospel.

PRAYER

Lord, God, in your Son you created a new humanity in which to praise and thank you for the work of salvation you wrought through him. Grant, we ask, that we may always live according to his spirit by striving to be reconciled with one another and seeing our neighbors as those you have chosen to complete the work of being formed after the image of your son. We asked this through Christ, our Lord. Amen.

GOSPEL

JESUS SAID TO HIS DISCIPLES:

"You have heard that it was said, *You shall love your neighbor and hate your enemy.* But I say to you, love your enemies, and pray for those who persecute you, that you may be children of your heavenly Father, for he makes his sun rise on the bad and the good, and causes rain to fall on the just and the unjust. For if you love those who love you, what recompense will you have? Do not the tax collectors do the same? And if you greet your brothers and sisters only, what is unusual about that? Do not the pagans do the same? So be perfect, just as your heavenly Father is perfect."

MATTHEW 5: 43-48

ST. JOHN OF THE CROSS

St. John of the Cross writes about a soul so transformed by God's love that he can ask God to forgive, just as Moses did. He describes those whom God has brought to the seventh step of perfection.

"The seventh step of the ladder [of love] gives it an ardent boldness. At this stage love neither profits by the judgment to wait nor makes use of the counsel to retreat, neither can it be curbed through shame. For the favor God now gives it imparts an ardent daring. Hence the Apostle says: Charity believes all things, hopes all things, and endures all things [1 Cor 13:7]. *Moses spoke from this step when he besought God to forgive the people or else strike his name out of the book of life [Ex 32:32]. These souls obtain from God what, with pleasure, they ask of him. David accordingly declares:* Delight in God, and he will grant you the petitions of

your heart [Ps 37:4]. *On this step the bride became bold and exclaimed:* Osculetur me osculo oris sui [Let him kiss me with the kiss of his mouth.] [Sg 1:1]. *It is illicit for the soul to become daring on this step if it does not perceive the divine favor of the king's scepter held out toward it [Est 5:2; 8:4], for it might then fall down the step it has already climbed. On these steps it must always conserve humility"* (N 2.20.2).

REFLECTION

It is easy to love those who love us. It is a lot harder to love those who do not love us. However, our Lord told us that unless we do love those who do not love us, we will not love as God our heavenly Father loves.

In this command to love, John of the Cross sees that we are called to grow continually in our love for God and neighbor. Love, in other words, is not static. It is not maintenance of the status quo but always moving us to go deeper in our love for God and others. Quoting Exodus 32:32, John of the Cross sees this love as moving us to beg God to forgive those with whom he is displeased. Quoting First Corinthians 13:7, God's love enables us to believe all things, hope all things, and endure all things. Finally, this love makes us dare to want to be loved by God in his kisses. While it is true that at this step, John of the Cross urges caution against going beyond what God will permit, it needs to be remembered that this was the seventh step of the ladder of love and that there are three more to go. Love knows no end of growing. It continues to grow in order to respond to God who is love.

PRAYER

God, our Father, you gave us your Son to be our teacher and model in living according to your way of doing things. Grant we ask, that we may so abide in your Spirit, that we may forgive those who offend us, with the same love with which you forgive us. We ask this through Christ, our Lord. Amen.

SECOND WEEK
OF
LENT

GOSPEL

Jesus took Peter, James, and John his brother, and led them up a high mountain by themselves. And he was transfigured before them; his face shone like the sun and his clothes became white as light. And behold, Moses and Elijah appeared to them, conversing with him. Then Peter said to Jesus in reply, "Lord, it is good that we are here. If you wish, I will make three tents here, one for you, one for Moses, and one for Elijah." While he was still speaking, behold, a bright cloud cast a shadow over them, then from the cloud came a voice that said, "This is my beloved Son, with whom I am well pleased; listen to him." When the disciples heard this, they fell prostrate and were very much afraid. But Jesus came and touched them, saying, "Rise, and do not be afraid." And when the disciples raised their eyes, they saw no one else but Jesus alone.

As they were coming down from the mountain, Jesus charged them, "Do not tell the vision to anyone until the Son of Man has been raised from the dead."

MATTHEW 17: 1-9

ST. JOHN OF THE CROSS

St. John of the Cross writes about the soul's need to undergo trials as it is transformed by the light of God.

"The trials that those who are to reach this state [the taste of eternal glory] *suffer are threefold: trials, discomforts, fears, and temptations from the world; and these in many ways: temptations, aridities, and afflictions in the senses; and tribulations, darknesses, distress, abandonment, temptations, and other trials in the spirit. In this way a soul is purified in its sensory and spiritual parts, as we mentioned in discussing the fourth verse of the first stanza.*

"The reason these trials are necessary in order to reach this state is that this highest union cannot be wrought in a soul that is not fortified by trials and temptations, and purified by tribulations, darknesses, and distress, just as a superior quality liqueur is poured only into a sturdy flask that is prepared and purified. By these trials the sensory part of the soul is purified and strengthened, and the spiritual part is refined, purged, and disposed. Since unpurified souls must undergo the sufferings of fire in the next life to attain union with God in glory, so in this life they must undergo the fire of these sufferings to reach the union of perfection. This fire acts on some more vigorously than on others, and on some for a longer time than on others, according to the degree of union to which God wishes to raise them, and according to what they must be purged of" (F 2.25).

REFLECTION

The goal of self-denial for John of the Cross is for the soul to become glorified in God. Just as Jesus, in doing the Father's will by accepting his will to suffer and die on the Cross became glorified in his Resurrection, so too the soul that follows Christ in the practice of denying its own gratification and accepting its sufferings becomes glorified in God.

In other words, trials strengthen us to bear the weight of God when he comes into us and make of us his dwelling place. Just as God in the three angels found rest under the tree while Abraham was ministering to him, so too does the Blessed Trinity find rest in those souls who do not seek their own gratification and embrace their own crosses.

PRAYER

God, our Father, you blessed the apostles of your Son with a vision of the glory that was to be his after his suffering and death so that they would be able to bear the scandal of his Cross. Grant, we ask, that we, while being similarly inspired, embrace our Lenten observance and our crosses in the hope of becoming transformed into your Son. We ask this through Christ, our Lord. Amen.

GOSPEL

Jesus took Peter, James and John and led them up a high mountain apart by themselves. And he was transfigured before them, and his clothes became dazzling white, such as no fuller on earth could bleach them. Then Elijah appeared to them along with Moses, and they were conversing with Jesus. Then Peter said to Jesus in reply, "Rabbi, it is good that we are here! Let us make three tents: one for you, one for Moses, and one for Elijah." He hardly knew what to say, they were so terrified. Then a cloud came, casting a shadow over them; from the cloud came a voice, "This is my beloved Son. Listen to him." Suddenly, looking around, they no longer saw anyone but Jesus alone with them.

As they were coming down from the mountain, he charged them not to relate what they had seen to anyone, except when the Son of Man had risen from the dead. So they kept the matter to themselves, questioning what rising from the dead meant.

MARK 9: 2-10

ST. JOHN OF THE CROSS

St. John of the Cross writes here about what the soul looks like when it is undergoing transformation into the light of God.

"All that can be said of this stanza [no. 3] is less than the reality, for the transformation of the soul in God is indescribable. Everything can be expressed in this statement: The soul becomes God from God through participation in him and in his attributes, which it terms the 'lamps of fire.'
in whose splendors

"To understand what these splendors of the lamps are and how the soul is resplendent in them, it should be known that they are the loving knowledge that the lamps of God's attributes give forth from themselves to the soul. United with them in its faculties, the soul is also resplendent like them, transformed in loving splendors.

"This illumination from the splendors, in which the soul shines brightly with the warmth of love, is not like that produced by material lamps that through their flames shed light round about them, but like the illumination that is within the very flames, for the soul is within these splendors. As a result it says, 'in whose splendors,' that is, within the splendors; and it does not merely mean 'within' but, as we pointed out, it means transformed in them. The soul is like the air within the flame, enkindled and transformed in the flame, for the flame is nothing but enkindled air. The movements and splendors of the flame are not from the air alone or from the fire of which the flame is composed, but from both air and fire. And the fire causes the air, which it has enkindled, to produce these same movements and splendors" (F 3.8c–9).

REFLECTION

When Jesus was transfigured in the light of his father, his humanity knew a love and peace that cannot be described. It was very short, but because it came from God, it left its mark in Jesus' humanity. It was the affirmation the Father gave to him as he embarked on a new phase of his ministry to journey to Jerusalem where he would be handed over to the Romans by his own people and put to death.

Christians, who respond to the call to follow Christ through Lent, and for that matter throughout their whole lives, are offered a chance to become transformed by the glory of God. If it is God's will, they become *like the air within the flame, enkindled and transformed in the flame.* While not all souls will know this experience equally, all have the potential for it as a result of Baptism.

Blessed are they who take seriously the Lord's calling to deny their very selves, take up their cross, and follow in his footsteps.

PRAYER

Lord, God, through the transfiguration of your Son, you blessed the human race with a foretaste of the glory that is to be its own as a result of your Son's acceptance of his death on the Cross. Grant, we ask, that we may conserve this hope in us, that we too will be transformed in like manner, by remaining faithful to our observance of Lent and embracing the cross you will for us. We ask this through Christ, our Lord. Amen.

GOSPEL

Jesus took Peter, John, and James and went up the mountain to pray. While he was praying his face changed in appearance and his clothing became dazzling white. And behold, two men were conversing with him, Moses and Elijah, who appeared in glory and spoke of his exodus that he was going to accomplish in Jerusalem. Peter and his companions had been overcome by sleep, but becoming fully awake, they saw his glory and the two men standing with him. As they were about to part from him, Peter said to Jesus, "Master, it is good that we are here; let us make three tents, one for you, one for Moses, and one for Elijah." But he did not know what he was saying. While he was still speaking, a cloud came and cast a shadow over them, and they became frightened when they entered the cloud. Then from the cloud came a voice that said, "This is my chosen Son; listen to him." After the voice had spoken, Jesus was found alone. They fell silent and did not at that time tell anyone what they had seen.

LUKE 9: 28B-36

ST. JOHN OF THE CROSS

St. John of the Cross writes about the soul's need to undergo a purification similar to that of wood being consumed by fire.

"For the sake of further clarity in this matter, we ought to note that this purgative and loving knowledge, or divine light we are speaking of, has the same effect on a soul that fire has on a log of wood. The soul is purged and prepared for union with the divine light just as the wood is prepared for transformation into the fire. Fire, when applied to wood, first dehumidifies it, dispelling all moisture and making it give off any water it contains. Then it gradually turns the wood black, makes it dark and

ugly, and even causes it to emit a bad odor. By drying out the wood, the fire brings to light and expels all those ugly and dark accidents that are contrary to fire. Finally, by heating and enkindling it from without, the fire transforms the wood into itself and makes it as beautiful as it is itself. Once transformed, the wood no longer has any activity or passivity of its own, except for its weight and its quantity that is denser than the fire. It possesses the properties and performs the actions of fire: It is dry and it dries; it is hot and it gives off heat; it is brilliant and it illumines; it is also much lighter in weight than before. It is the fire that produces all these properties in the wood" (N 2.10.1).

REFLECTION

The purification that John of the Cross writes about here is the one where God takes a person from the bottom of himself or herself and makes him or her like himself. John of the Cross likens it to wood being taken from the core of itself by fire, in order to be made like the fire.

In today's Gospel, Jesus was transfigured by the light of the Father, an experience human beings never had before, but now becomes available to them when they follow Jesus, imitate his way of life, and accept crosses in love for him. These crosses are the means by which God strengthens us for the hour he alone knows, when he will take us at the core of our being, and make us like himself, in much the same way fire works on wood.

PRAYER

God, our Father, you revealed the glory of your Son on Mount Tabor, so that his disciples would not lose faith when Jesus dies on the Cross. Grant, we ask, that in conserving in memory the mysteries of your Son, we may experience these mysteries in our own lives and so be lead to share in the glory of the Resurrection. Amen.

GOSPEL

JESUS SAID TO HIS DISCIPLES:

"Be merciful, just as your Father is merciful.

"Stop judging and you will not be judged. Stop condemning and you will not be condemned. Forgive and you will be forgiven. Give and gifts will be given to you; a good measure, packed together, shaken down, and overflowing, will be poured into your lap. For the measure with which you measure will in return be measured out to you."

LUKE 6: 36-38

ST. JOHN OF THE CROSS

Near the end of his life, St. John of the Cross was persecuted by the governing members of his order. He wrote a letter during that period consoling an unknown person who was also being persecuted.

"Have a great love for those who contradict and fail to love you, for in this way love is begotten in a heart that has no love. God so acts with us, for he loves us that we might love by means of the very love he bears toward us" (L 33, October–November 1591).

REFLECTION

On Saturday of the First Week of Lent, we heard in Matthew 5:43–48; that we were to love not only those who love us, but even our enemies. Jesus told us that we had to be perfect as our heavenly Father is perfect. In today's Gospel, Jesus tells us to be merciful as our heavenly Father is merciful, by not judging or condemning others, but by forgiving others as God has forgiven us.

In his lifetime, John of the Cross experienced two periods of persecution. The first took place when he was confessor for the nuns in Avila and he was kidnapped by the friars and held prisoner for ten months. The second time was when he was being hunted down by a fellow friar who wanted to throw him out of the order. From these experiences, John of the Cross learned how to profit spiritually. He learned that if allowed to grow, love will transform us into the love of God who is love.

PRAYER

God, our Father, in the life of your Son you gave us an example of patience and forbearance with those who persecute us. Grant, we ask, that we may have the same patience and forbearance he had and so come to experience the power of your overflowing love for us. We ask this through Christ, our Lord. Amen.

GOSPEL

Jesus spoke to the crowds and to his disciples, saying, "The scribes and the Pharisees have taken their seat on the chair of Moses. Therefore, do and observe all things whatsoever they tell you, but do not follow their example. For they preach but they do not practice. They tie up heavy burdens hard to carry and lay them on people's shoulders, but they will not lift a finger to move them. All their works are performed to be seen. They widen their phylacteries and lengthen their tassels. They love places of honor at banquets, seats of honor in synagogues, greetings in marketplaces, and the salutation 'Rabbi.' As for you, do not be called 'Rabbi.' You have but one teacher, and you are all brothers. Call no one on earth your father; you have but one Father in heaven. Do not be called 'Master'; you have but one master, the Christ. The greatest among you must be your servant. Whoever exalts himself will be humbled; but whoever humbles himself will be exalted."

MATTHEW 23: 1-12

ST. JOHN OF THE CROSS

For John of the Cross, as for all great spiritual writers, humility—true self-knowledge—is the foundation of spiritual growth.

"To practice the third counsel [for reaching perfection], *which concerns the practice of virtue, you should be constant in your religious observance and in obedience without any concern for the world, but only for God. In order to achieve this and avoid being deceived, you should never set your eyes on the satisfaction or dissatisfaction of the work at hand as a motive for doing it or failing to do it, but on doing it for God. Thus you must undertake all things, agreeable or disagreeable, for the sole purpose of pleasing God through them.*

"To do this with fortitude and constancy and acquire the virtues quickly, you should take care always to be inclined to the difficult more than to the easy, to the rugged more than to the soft, to the hard and distasteful in a work more than to its delightful and pleasant aspects; and do not go about choosing what is less a cross, for the cross is a light burden [Mt 11:30]. *The heavier a burden is, the lighter it becomes when borne for Christ.*

"You should try, too, by taking the lowest place always, that in things bringing comfort to your brothers in religion they be preferred to you. This you should do wholeheartedly, for it is the way to becoming greater in spiritual things, as God tells us in his Gospel: . . . [Whoever humbles himself will be exalted.] [Mt 23:12]" (CO 5–6).

REFLECTION

Humility is not a popular word today. It is rare to hear being called "humble" as a compliment, although, a close equivalent is "down-to-earth" or "unpretentious."

John of the Cross has another understanding in mind, which is the self-knowledge of knowing all that is good in oneself comes from God and all that is wicked from oneself.

Growing into this kind of self-knowledge takes time and John of the Cross provides a way in which this can be achieved: taking on the chores of life that are less gratifying, not focusing on a work because it is pleasing but because it can be done for God, and seeking to bring comfort to others. Here you have the whole program of the spiritual life of John of the Cross. Those who bend themselves to follow Christ and imitate him will be exalted as he was. Promise!

PRAYER

Lord, God, through this Season of Lent, you call us to foster within ourselves a spirit of humility in imitation of your Son through the disciplines of fasting, prayer, and almsgiving. Grant, we ask, that we may be preserved from the temptation of pride in our accomplishments so that we may be true coheirs with Christ, the firstborn of many brothers and sisters. We ask this in His name. Amen.

GOSPEL

As Jesus was going up to Jerusalem, he took the Twelve disciples aside by themselves, and said to them on the way, "Behold, we are going up to Jerusalem, and the Son of Man will be handed over to the chief priests and the scribes, and they will condemn him to death, and hand him over to the Gentiles to be mocked and scourged and crucified, and he will be raised on the third day."

Then the mother of the sons of Zebedee approached Jesus with her sons and did him homage, wishing to ask him for something. He said to her, "What do you wish?" She answered him, "Command that these two sons of mine sit, one at your right and the other at your left, in your kingdom." Jesus said in reply, "You do not know what you are asking. Can you drink the chalice that I am going to drink?" They said to him, "We can." He replied, "My chalice you will indeed drink, but to sit at my right and at my left, this is not mine to give but is for those for whom it has been prepared by my Father." When the ten heard this, they became indignant at the two brothers. But Jesus summoned them and said, "You know that the rulers of the Gentiles lord it over them, and the great ones make their authority over them felt. But it shall not be so among you. Rather, whoever wishes to be great among you shall be your servant; whoever wishes to be first among you shall be your slave. Just so, the Son of Man did not come to be served but to serve and to give his life as a ransom for many."

MATTHEW 20: 17-28

ST. JOHN OF THE CROSS

In his work, the Ascent of Mount Carmel, John of the Cross illustrates his teaching that union with God is arrived at through self-denying imitation of Christ.

"Oh, who can explain the extent of the denial our Lord wishes of us! This negation must be similar to a temporal, natural, and spiritual death in all things; that is, with regard to the esteem the will has for them. It is in the will that all negation takes place. Our Savior referred to this when he declared: Whoever wishes to save his life will lose it *(Those who want to possess something, or seek it for self, will lose it);* and whoever loses his soul for my sake will gain it *[Mt 16:25; Lk 9:24]. This latter means: Those who renounce for Christ all that their wills can both desire and enjoy by choosing what bears closer resemblance to the cross—which in St. John our Lord terms hating one's own soul [Jn 12:25]—these same will gain it.*

"His Majesty taught this to those two disciples who came to ask him for places at his right and left. Without responding to their request for glory, he offered them the chalice he was about to drink as something safer and more precious on this earth than enjoyment [Mt 20:22].

"This chalice means death to one's natural self through denudation and annihilation. By this means one is able to walk along the narrow path in the sensitive part of the soul, as we said, and in the spiritual part (as we will now say), in one's understanding, joy, and feeling. Accordingly, a person can attain to dispossession in both parts of the soul. Not only this, but even in the spirit one will be unhindered in one's journey on the narrow road. For on this road there is room only for self-denial (as our Savior asserts) and the cross. The cross is a supporting staff and greatly lightens and eases the journey" (A 2.7.6–7a).

REFLECTION

Over the centuries, many have found John of the Cross hard to take and John of the Cross had no illusion that his teaching would be hard to take. However, as far as he was concerned, it was not his teaching. It was the teaching of Christ, no more and no less. Just as Christ found it hard to help James and John to understand what true discipleship meant, so too has the Holy Spirit found it hard to find souls who truly want to follow Christ. One day I came across a statement that even in the most Christian eras, only 9 percent of the population was truly trying to follow Christ. Yes. John of the Cross is demanding; but so too is the Gospel.

PRAYER

God, our Father, you sent your Son to live out our human condition of suffering and death so that we may be made partakers of your divine nature. Grant, we ask, that we too may have the courage to embrace the sufferings and many "deaths" of our lives so that we may share in the glory of your Son's Resurrection. We ask this in His name. Amen.

GOSPEL

JESUS SAID TO THE PHARISEES:

"There was a rich man who dressed in purple garments and fine linen and dined sumptuously each day. And lying at his door was a poor man named Lazarus, covered with sores, who would gladly have eaten his fill of the scraps that fell from the rich man's table. Dogs even used to come and lick his sores. When the poor man died, he was carried away by angels to the bosom of Abraham. The rich man also died and was buried, and from the netherworld, where he was in torment, he raised his eyes and saw Abraham far off and Lazarus at his side. And he cried out, 'Father Abraham, have pity on me. Send Lazarus to dip the tip of his finger in water and cool my tongue, for I am suffering torment in these flames.' Abraham replied, 'My child, remember that you received what was good during your lifetime while Lazarus likewise received what was bad; but now he is comforted here, whereas you are tormented. Moreover, between us and you a great chasm is established to prevent anyone from crossing who might wish to go from our side to yours or from your side to ours.' He said, 'Then I beg you, father, send him to my father's house, for I have five brothers, so that he may warn them, lest they too come to this place of torment.' But Abraham replied, 'They have Moses and the prophets. Let them listen to them.' He said, 'Oh no, father Abraham, but if someone from the dead goes to them, they will repent.' Then Abraham said, 'If they will not listen to Moses and the prophets, neither will they be persuaded if someone should rise from the dead.'"

LUKE 16: 19-31

ST. JOHN OF THE CROSS

Here John of the Cross cites Divine Wisdom in the book of Proverbs.

"Divine Wisdom, with pity for these souls that become ugly, abject, miserable, and poor because of their love for worldly things, which in their opinion are rich and beautiful, exclaims in Proverbs: . . . O people, I cry to you, my voice is directed to the children of this earth. Be attentive, little ones, to cunning and sagacity; and you ignorant, be careful. Listen, because I want to speak of great things. Riches and glory are mine, high riches and justice. The fruit you will find in me is better than gold and precious stones; and my generations (what will be engendered of me in your souls) are better than choice silver. I walk along the ways of justice, in the midst of the paths of judgment, to enrich those who love me and to fill their treasures completely [Prv. 8:4–6, 18–21].

"Divine Wisdom speaks, here, to all those who are attached to the things of the world. She calls them little ones because they become as little as the things they love. She tells them, accordingly, to be cunning and careful, that she is dealing with great things, not small things, as they are; and that the riches and glory they love are with her and in her, not where they think; and that lofty riches and justice are present in her. Although in their opinion the things of this world are riches, she tells them to bear in mind that her riches are more precious, that the fruit found in them will be better than gold and precious stones, and that what she begets in souls has greater value than cherished silver, which signifies every kind of affection possible in this life" (A 1.4.8).

REFLECTION

We live in a world that offers us new and exciting technological inventions that make our lives easier in a way that would have been unimaginable even twenty years ago. While these are all good, and now necessary, they can become a new source of inordinate desire. For example, many people are addicted to being on the Internet. Others feel the need to always be in touch with somebody. More and more, one's awareness becomes centered on one's personal problems or the problems of one's friends. Meanwhile, there are those who are right in front of us just grateful for a kind word.

The problem with these new inventions is not that they exist but rather our desire for them. The more we desire them, the less we keep the mouth of our desire open for God alone. The more we become focused on them, the less we are able to see the needs of our immediate neighbors. We become like the rich man in today's Gospel who was so in love with his own comfort that he could not recognize Lazarus lying at his door.

Just as it was in Jesus' day and in John of the Cross' day, so too in our day we can become so focused on our inventions (and the comfort they afford) that we become like them and fail to see the riches that the divine wisdom in Christ alone offers us.

PRAYER

Lord, God, you have called us to be the stewards of this earth's goods for the good of others and our own. Grant, we ask, that we may not set our hearts on these, but on your Son and his wisdom, so that we may be able respond to the needs of others and thus merit being made coheirs with Him. We ask this in His name. Amen.

GOSPEL

JESUS SAID TO THE CHIEF PRIESTS AND
THE ELDERS OF THE PEOPLE:

"Hear another parable. There was a landowner who planted a vineyard, put a hedge around it, dug a wine press in it, and built a tower. Then he leased it to tenants and went on a journey. When vintage time drew near, he sent his servants to the tenants to obtain his produce. But the tenants seized the servants and one they beat, another they killed, and a third they stoned. Again he sent other servants, more numerous than the first ones, but they treated them in the same way. Finally, he sent his son to them, thinking, 'They will respect my son.' But when the tenants saw the son, they said to one another, 'This is the heir. Come, let us kill him and acquire his inheritance.' They seized him, threw him out of the vineyard, and killed him. What will the owner of the vineyard do to those tenants when he comes?" They answered him, "He will put those wretched men to a wretched death and lease his vineyard to other tenants who will give him the produce at the proper times." Jesus said to them, "Did you never read in the Scriptures:

The stone that the builders rejected
has become the cornerstone;
by the Lord has this been done,
and it is wonderful in our eyes?

Therefore, I say to you, the Kingdom of God will be taken away from you and given to a people that will produce its fruit."

When the chief priests and the Pharisees heard his parables, they knew that he was speaking about them. And although they were attempting to arrest him, they feared the crowds, for they regarded him as a prophet.

MATTHEW 21: 33-43, 45-46

ST. JOHN OF THE CROSS

St. John of the Cross writes at great length about the "harm resulting from joy of will in temporal goods."

"The third degree of this privative harm is the complete abandoning of God. These individuals don't care about observing God's law, but attend to worldly goods and allow themselves to fall into mortal sins through covetousness. This third degree is indicated in the next assertion of this passage from Exodus: He forsook God his Maker [Dt 32:15]. *This degree includes all who are so engrossed in the things, riches, and affairs of this world that they care nothing about fulfilling the obligations of God's law. Forgetful and sluggish about matters pertaining to their salvation, they become much more alive and astute in the things of the world—so much so that Christ in the Gospel calls them children of this world. He says they are more prudent and keen in their affairs than the children of light are in theirs [Lk 16:8]. Thus in the affairs of God they are nothing, and in those of the world they are everything. These, precisely, are the greedy. Their appetite and joy are already so extended and dispersed among creatures—and with such anxiety—that they cannot be satisfied. Rather, their appetite and thirst increase more as they regress further from God, the fount that alone can satisfy them. To these individuals God refers through Jeremiah:* They have abandoned me, the fount of living water, and dug for themselves leaking cisterns that cannot hold water [Jer 2:13]. *The reason for this dissatisfaction is that creatures do not slake the thirst of the avaricious, but rather intensify it.*

"These greedy persons fall into thousands of kinds of sins out of love for temporal goods, and the harm they suffer is indeterminable. David says of them: Transierunt in affectum cordis [Ps 73:7]*" (A 3.19.7).*

REFLECTION

As John of the Cross noted, there is a harm that comes from finding joy in temporal goods. It is clear from today's Gospel that the workers of the vineyard went from finding joy in working for the landowner to wanting the vineyard for themselves. They found their joy in the wealth and status that the vineyard gave them. This in turn led them to forsake the landowner who in the parable represents God. Similarly, Jesus accuses the chief priests and Pharisees of the fault of forgetting God, which kept them from seeing Jesus as the Son of God.

Even though we as Christians have been blessed with the sacraments of initiation and the example of Christ, we too can be tempted to find our joy in temporal goods and forget God. We too can become so obsessed with possessing them that we are trapped and possessed by them. Thus, we must strive to be detached in our attitude toward things so that we may achieve that liberality of spirit John of the Cross describes.

PRAYER

Lord, God, you have called us to follow your Son with a heart focused on him and his teaching alone during this Season of Lent. Grant, we ask, that we may be freed from the self-love and self-seeking we glory in by having the temporal goods of this life, so that we may receive them with open hands from you; and use them with free hearts centered on you. We ask this in Christ, your Son's name. Amen.

GOSPEL

Tax collectors and sinners were all drawing near to listen to Jesus, but the Pharisees and scribes began to complain, saying, "This man welcomes sinners and eats with them." So to them Jesus addressed this parable. "A man had two sons, and the younger son said to his father, 'Father, give me the share of your estate that should come to me.' So the father divided the property between them. After a few days, the younger son collected all his belongings and set off to a distant country where he squandered his inheritance on a life of dissipation. When he had freely spent everything, a severe famine struck that country, and he found himself in dire need. So he hired himself out to one of the local citizens who sent him to his farm to tend the swine. And he longed to eat his fill of the pods on which the swine fed, but nobody gave him any. Coming to his senses he thought, 'How many of my father's hired workers have more than enough food to eat, but here am I, dying from hunger. I shall get up and go to my father and I shall say to him, "Father, I have sinned against heaven and against you. I no longer deserve to be called your son; treat me as you would treat one of your hired workers."' So he got up and went back to his father. While he was still a long way off, his father caught sight of him, and was filled with compassion. He ran to his son, embraced him and kissed him. His son said to him, 'Father, I have sinned against heaven and against you; I no longer deserve to be called your son.' But his father ordered his servants, 'Quickly, bring the finest robe and put it on him; put a ring on his finger and sandals on his feet. Take the fattened calf and slaughter it. Then let us celebrate with a feast, because this son of mine was dead, and has come to life again; he was lost, and has been found.' Then the celebration began. Now the older son had been out in the field and, on his way back, as he neared the house, he heard the sound of music and dancing. He called one of the servants and asked what this might mean. The servant said to him, 'Your brother has returned and your father has slaughtered the fattened calf because he has him back safe and sound.' He became angry, and when he refused to enter the house, his father came out and pleaded with him. He said to his father in reply, 'Look, all these years I served you and not once did I disobey your orders; yet you never gave me even a young goat to feast on with my friends. But when your son returns who swallowed up your property with prostitutes, for him you slaughter the fattened calf.' He said to him, 'My son, you are here with me always; everything I have is yours. But now we must celebrate and rejoice, because your brother was dead and has come to life again; he was lost and has been found.'"

LUKE 15: 1-3, 11-32

ST. JOHN OF THE CROSS

Here John of the Cross touches on the pride of spirit that exists in beginners in the spiritual life that is like the older brother's pride that he has when he paraded his good works before his father.

"These beginners feel so fervent and diligent in their spiritual exercises and undertakings that a certain kind of secret pride is generated in them that begets a complacency with themselves and their accomplishments, even though holy works do of their very nature cause humility. Then they develop a somewhat vain—at times very vain—desire to speak of spiritual things in others' presence, and sometimes even to instruct rather than be instructed; in their hearts they condemn others who do not seem to have the kind of devotion they would like them to have, and sometimes they give expression to this criticism like the pharisee who despised the publican while he boasted and praised God for the good deeds he himself accomplished" [Lk 18:11–12](N 1.2.1).

REFLECTION

What John of the Cross says of beginners could be applied to the elder son. Like them, the elder son developed a secret pride in being fervent and diligent in his work for his father. He even kept a record of it: *Look, all these years I served you and not once did I disobey your orders.* This should cause us to pause and reflect on "the good work" we do for our Lord. Are we really selfless in our work? Do we want to be appreciated by our Lord? By others? Or, do we compare ourselves with others and say, "I am not as bad as so and so," or, "at least I go to Mass." and the like.

John of the Cross describes these attitudes as those of beginners in the spiritual life. Even though they may have been at it for a long time, and have mastered the rudiments of meditation, spiritual reading, journaling, and the like, they are still beginners. They still suffer from taking pride in their spiritual accomplishments.

Lent is a time to grow in self-knowledge. The Gospel reading and John of the Cross encourage us to see ourselves as God sees us and turn to our Lord for forgiveness and healing.

PRAYER

Lord God, your Son entered into the human scene of sin and weakness in order to free us from these and so enable us to enter into fellowship with you. Grant, we ask, that we not be quick to fault the shortcomings of others, since you came to heal them of these and our own. We ask this through Christ, your Son. Amen.

THIRD WEEK
OF
LENT

GOSPEL

Jesus came to a town of Samaria called Sychar, near the plot of land that Jacob had given to his son Joseph. Jacob's well was there. Jesus, tired from his journey, sat down there at the well. It was about noon.

A woman of Samaria came to draw water. Jesus said to her, "Give me a drink." His disciples had gone into the town to buy food. The Samaritan woman said to him, "How can you, a Jew, ask me, a Samaritan woman, for a drink?" — For Jews use nothing in common with Samaritans. — Jesus answered and said to her, "If you knew the gift of God and who is saying to you, 'Give me a drink,' you would have asked him and he would have given you living water." The woman said to him, "Sir, you do not even have a bucket and the cistern is deep; where then can you get this living water? Are you greater than our father Jacob, who gave us this cistern and drank from it himself with his children and his flocks?" Jesus answered and said to her, "Everyone who drinks this water will be thirsty again; but whoever drinks the water I shall give will never thirst; the water I shall give will become in him a spring of water welling up to eternal life." The woman said to him, "Sir, give me this water, so that I may not be thirsty or have to keep coming here to draw water."

Jesus said to her, "Go call your husband and come back." The woman answered and said to him, "I do not have a husband." Jesus answered her, "You are right in saying, 'I do not have a husband.' For you have had five husbands, and the one you have now is not your husband. What you have said is true." The woman said to him, "Sir, I can see that you are a prophet. Our ancestors worshiped on this mountain; but you people say that the place to worship is in Jerusalem." Jesus said to her, "Believe me, woman, the hour is coming when you will worship the Father neither on this mountain nor in Jerusalem. You people worship what you do not understand; we worship what we understand, because salvation is from the Jews. But the hour is coming, and is now here, when true worshipers will worship the Father in Spirit and truth; and indeed the

Father seeks such people to worship him. God is Spirit, and those who worship him must worship in Spirit and truth." The woman said to him, "I know that the Messiah is coming, the one called the Christ; when he comes, he will tell us everything." Jesus said to her, "I am he, the one speaking with you."

At that moment his disciples returned, and were amazed that he was talking with a woman, but still no one said, "What are you looking for?" or "Why are you talking with her?" The woman left her water jar and went into the town and said to the people, "Come see a man who told me everything I have done. Could he possibly be the Christ?" They went out of the town and came to him. Meanwhile, the disciples urged him, "Rabbi, eat." But he said to them, "I have food to eat of which you do not know." So the disciples said to one another, "Could someone have brought him something to eat?" Jesus said to them, "My food is to do the will of the one who sent me and to finish his work. Do you not say, 'In four months the harvest will be here'? I tell you, look up and see the fields ripe for the harvest. The reaper is already receiving payment and gathering crops for eternal life, so that the sower and reaper can rejoice together. For here the saying is verified that 'One sows and another reaps.' I sent you to reap what you have not worked for; others have done the work, and you are sharing the fruits of their work."

Many of the Samaritans of that town began to believe in him because of the word of the woman who testified, "He told me everything I have done." When the Samaritans came to him, they invited him to stay with them; and he stayed there two days. Many more began to believe in him because of his word, and they said to the woman, "We no longer believe because of your word; for we have heard for ourselves, and we know that this is truly the savior of the world."

JOHN 4: 5-42

Shorter form: JOHN 4:5-15, 19b-26, 39a, 40-42
Longer form may be optionally read on any day in the third week of Lent

ST. JOHN OF THE CROSS

Here John of the Cross has an interesting take on why the Samaritan woman left her water jar behind. If she, who was a sinner, could be so inflamed by the Word of Christ, what keeps those of us who have believed for years from being so?

"This is the language and these the words God speaks in souls that are purged, cleansed, and all enkindled; as David exclaimed: Your word is exceedingly enkindled *[Ps 119:139];* and the prophet: Are not my words, perchance, like a fire? *[Jer 23:29].* As God himself says through St. John, these words are spirit and life *[Jn 6:63].* These words are perceived by souls who have ears to hear them, those souls, as I say, that are cleansed and enamored. Those who do not have a sound palate, but seek other tastes, cannot taste the spirit and life of God's words; his words, rather, are distasteful to them.*

"Hence the loftier were the words of the Son of God, the more taste-less they were to the impure, as happened when he preached the sovereign and loving doctrine of the Holy Eucharist, for many turned away [Jn. 6:60–61, 66].

"Those who do not relish this language God speaks within them must not think on this account that others do not taste it. St. Peter tasted it in his soul when he said to Christ: Lord, where shall we go? You have the words of eternal life *[Jn. 6:68].* And the Samaritan woman forgot the water and the water jar for the sweetness of God's words *[Jn 4:28].*

"Since this soul is so close to God that it is transformed into a flame of love in which the Father, the Son, and the Holy Spirit are communicated to it, how can it be thought incredible that it enjoy a foretaste of eternal life? Yet it does not enjoy eternal life perfectly since the conditions of this life do not allow it. But the delight that the flaring of the Holy Spirit generates in the soul is so sublime that it makes it know that which savors of eternal life. Thus it refers to this flame as living, not because the flame is not always living but because of this effect; it makes the soul live in God spiritually and experience the life of God in the manner David mentions:

My heart and my flesh rejoiced in the living God [Ps 84:2]. *David did not refer to God as living because of a necessity to do so, for God is always living, but in order to manifest that the spirit and the senses, transformed in God, enjoy him in a living way, which is to taste the living God—that is, God's life, eternal life. Nor did David call him the living God other than because he enjoyed him in a living way, although not perfectly, but as though by a glimpse of eternal life. Thus in this flame the soul experiences God so vividly and tastes him with such delight and sweetness"* (F 1.5–6).

REFLECTION

At Christmas, the Word of God was made flesh and made his dwelling upon us. Ever since then his word has been available to us to grow in our capacity to encounter God through him.

When the Samaritan woman at the well first met Jesus, she thought of him as a stranger, then a Jew, then a man whom she called sir, then a prophet, and finally, she suspected him to be the Messiah. The more she spoke with him the more she became opened to the mystery of the Word Incarnate in Jesus.

John of the Cross reflecting on the Samaritan woman's experience saw her as having the language of God spoken within her. He invites us in turn to hear the same language in ourselves. Along with fasting and almsgiving we are called to pray. To spend time today and pray after Mass is a good way to begin hearing the silent language of God's love within you.

PRAYER

O Lord, your Word opened up the vista of salvation to the Samaritan woman who was ostracized from her own community. Grant, we ask, that we may grow in devotion to you the Word of God, so that like her we too may become inflamed with your Spirit and so worship your Father in Spirit and in You the Truth. We ask this in your name. Amen.

GOSPEL

Since the Passover of the Jews was near, Jesus went up to Jerusalem. He found in the temple area those who had sold oxen, sheep and doves, as well as the money changers seated there. He made a whip out of cords and drove them all out of the temple area, with sheep and oxen, and spilled the coins of the money changers and overturned their tables, and to those who sold doves he said, "Take these out of here, and stop making my Father's house a marketplace." His disciples recalled the words of Scripture, *Zeal for your house will consume me.* At this the Jews answered and said to him, "What sign can you show us for doing this?" Jesus answered and said to them, "Destroy this temple and in three days I will raise it up." The Jews said, "This temple has been under construction for forty-six years, and you will raise it up in three days?" But he was speaking about the temple of his body. Therefore, when he was raised from the dead, his disciples remembered that he had said this, and they came to believe the Scripture and the word Jesus had spoken.

While he was in Jerusalem for the feast of Passover, many began to believe in his name when they saw the signs he was doing. But Jesus would not trust himself to them because he knew them all, and did not need anyone to testify about human nature. He himself understood it well.

JOHN 2: 13-25

ST. JOHN OF THE CROSS

John of the Cross strongly opposes seeking signs because they are in fact, a sign of a lack of faith.

"God never works these marvels except when they are a necessity for believing. Lest his disciples go without merit by having sensible proof of his Resurrection, he did many things to further their belief before they saw him. Mary Magdalene was first shown the empty sepulcher, and afterward the angels told her about the Resurrection so she would, by hearing, believe before seeing. As St. Paul says: Faith comes through hearing [Rom 10:17]. *And though she beheld him, he seemed only an ordinary man, so by the warmth of his presence he could finish instructing her in the belief she was lacking* [Mt 28:1–6; Lk 24:4–10; Jn 20:11–18]. *And the women were sent to tell the disciples first; then these disciples set out to see the sepulcher* [Mt. 28:7–8]. *And journeying incognito to Emmaus with two of his followers, he inflamed their hearts in faith before allowing them to see* [Lk 24:15–32]. *Finally he reproved all his disciples for refusing to believe those who had told them of his Resurrection* [Mk 16:14]. *And announcing to St. Thomas that they are blessed who believe without seeing, he reprimanded him for desiring to experience the sight and touch of his wounds* [Jn 20:25, 29].

"Thus God is not inclined to work miracles. When he works them he does so, as they say, out of necessity. He consequently reprimanded the pharisees because they would not give assent without signs: If you do not see signs and wonders, you do not believe [Jn 4:48]. *Those, then, who love to rejoice in these supernatural works suffer a great loss in faith"* (A 3.31.8d–9).

REFLECTION

A man who has been dating a woman for a long time may seek a sign from her that she would be interested in marrying him. A young man feeling an attraction to the priesthood may seek a sign that God is indeed calling him to the priesthood. A young woman feeling attracted to religious life may seek a sign from God that God is indeed calling her to a particular community.

Seeking these signs is just. What our Lord teaches against is the seeking of extraordinary signs when God has already given enough signs for his contemporaries to believe in him. The same is true with John of the Cross. Too often Christians seek signs from God when clearly only faith will do. They believe that the Christian life is a matter of signs and wonders when all that God asks of them is faith and the fulfillment of their duties in life. As John of the Cross wrote to Dona Juana de Pedreza:

"What is it you desire? What kind of life or method of procedure do you paint for yourself in this life? What do you think serving God involves other than avoiding evil, keeping his commandments, and being occupied with the things of God as best we can? When this is had, what need is there of other apprehensions or other lights and satisfactions from this source or that?" (L 19c, October 12, 1589).

PRAYER

God, our Father, each week you renew the faith of your people through the Body and Blood of your Son through the signs of bread and wine. Grant, we ask, that through the discipline of Lent, we may continue to appreciate your presence through these signs and thus be freed from seeking you in extraordinary ones. We ask this through Christ, your Son and our Lord. Amen.

GOSPEL

Some people told Jesus about the Galileans whose blood Pilate had mingled with the blood of their sacrifices. Jesus said to them in reply, "Do you think that because these Galileans suffered in this way they were greater sinners than all other Galileans? By no means! But I tell you, if you do not repent, you will all perish as they did! Or those eighteen people who were killed when the tower at Siloam fell on them – do you think they were more guilty than everyone else who lived in Jerusalem? By no means! But I tell you, if you do not repent, you will all perish as they did!"

And he told them this parable: "There once was a person who had a fig tree planted in his orchard, and when he came in search of fruit on it but found none, he said to the gardener, 'For three years now I have come in search of fruit on this fig tree but have found none. So cut it down. Why should it exhaust the soil?' He said to him in reply, 'Sir, leave it for this year also, and I shall cultivate the ground around it and fertilize it; it may bear fruit in the future. If not you can cut it down.'"

LUKE 13: 1-9

ST. JOHN OF THE CROSS

When John of the Cross writes about repentance, he is very thorough.

"Those desiring to climb to the summit of the mount in order to become an altar for the offering of a sacrifice of pure love and praise and reverence to God must first accomplish these three tasks perfectly. First, they must cast out strange gods, all alien affections and attachments. Second, by denying these appetites and repenting of them—through the dark night of the senses—they must purify themselves of the residue. Third, in order

to reach the top of this high mount, their garments must be changed. By means of the first two works, God will substitute new garments for the old. The soul will be clothed in a new understanding of God in God (through removal of the old understanding) and in a new love of God in God, once the will is stripped of all the old cravings and satisfactions. And God will vest the soul with new knowledge when the other old ideas and images are cast aside [Col 3:9]. He causes all that is of the old self, the abilities of one's natural being, to cease, and he attires all the faculties with new supernatural abilities. As a result, one's activities, once human, now become divine. This is achieved in the state of union when the soul, in which God alone dwells, has no other function than that of an altar on which God is adored in praise and love.

"God commanded that the altar of the Ark of the Covenant be empty and hollow [Ex 27:8] to remind the soul how void of all things God wishes it to be if it is to serve as a worthy dwelling for His Majesty. It was forbidden that the altar have any strange fire, or that its own go out; so much so that when Nadab and Abihu, the sons of the high priest Aaron, offered strange fire on our Lord's altar God became angry and slew them there in front of the altar [Lv 10:1–2]. *The lesson we derive here is that one's love for God must never fail or be mixed with alien loves if one wants to be a worthy altar of sacrifice.* [my emphasis]" (A 1.5.7).

REFLECTION

From time to time we hear the lament that Catholics are not going to confession as much as they used to. Maybe in some way this is good as it shows that Catholics have moved away from confessing minor faults and venial sins. On the other hand, it may be something serious. It may be a sign that we as Catholics have lost our way in knowing how we stand before God. Maybe we have lost knowing how to examine our conscience and our knowledge of who we are.

The selection from John of the Cross challenges us to grow in self-knowledge. While it is true that we do not worship false gods of the past, we may have some new ones. For example, how much time and money do we spend for things other than God? or, how much time and energy do we spend for products or services that we cannot afford? Asking ourselves these types of questions can further us along the path of conversion that our Lord calls us to travel today.

PRAYER

Lord, God, through the Season of Lent, you call us to conduct a spiritual spring-cleaning of all that we find within us that is not of you, through prayer, fasting, and self-denial. Grant, we ask, that we may continue to persevere in this work so that when Holy Week arrives, we may be able join in spirit with your Son who will climb the mountain of his gift of self to you through his crucifixion. We ask this through Christ, our Lord. Amen.

GOSPEL

JESUS SAID TO THE PEOPLE IN THE SYNAGOGUE
AT NAZARETH:

"Amen, I say to you, no prophet is accepted in his own native place. Indeed, I tell you, there were many widows in Israel in the days of Elijah when the sky was closed for three and a half years and a severe famine spread over the entire land. It was to none of these that Elijah was sent, but only to a widow in Zarephath in the land of Sidon. Again, there were many lepers in Israel during the time of Elisha the prophet; yet not one of them was cleansed, but only Naaman the Syrian." When the people in the synagogue heard this, they were all filled with fury. They rose up, drove him out of the town, and led him to the brow of the hill on which their town had been built, to hurl him down headlong. But he passed through the midst of them and went away.

LUKE 4: 24-30

ST. JOHN OF THE CROSS

John of the Cross gives a powerful description of the rejection our Lord endured from his own people and from God the Father.

"Second, at the moment of his death he was certainly annihilated in his soul, without any consolation or relief, since the Father had left him that way in innermost aridity in the lower part. He was thereby compelled to cry out: My God, My God, why have you forsaken me? [Mt 27:46]. *This was the most extreme abandonment, sensitively, that he had suffered in his life. And by it he accomplished the most marvelous work of his whole life, surpassing all the works and deeds and miracles that he had ever performed on earth or in heaven. That is, he brought about the reconciliation and union of the human race with God through grace. The Lord achieved this, as I say, at the moment in which he was most annihilated in all things: in his reputation before people, since in watching him die they mocked him instead of esteeming him; in his human nature, by dying; and in spiritual help and consolation from his Father, for he was forsaken by his Father at that time, annihilated and reduced to nothing, so as to pay the debt fully and bring people to union with God. David says of him:* Ad nihilum redactus sum et nescivi [Ps 73:22], *that those who are truly spiritual might understand the mystery of the door and way (which is Christ) leading to union with God, and that they might realize that their union with God and the greatness of the work they accomplish will be measured by their annihilation of themselves for God in the sensory and spiritual parts of their souls. When they are reduced to nothing, the highest degree of humility, the spiritual union between their souls and God will be an accomplished fact. This union is the most noble and sublime state attainable in this life. The journey, then, does not consist in consolations, delights, and spiritual feelings, but in the living death of the cross, sensory and spiritual, exterior and interior. [my emphasis]"* (A 2.7.11).

REFLECTION

Every so often, we see something like the top ten celebrities, the top ten sports heroes and so forth. We live in a world where everyone strives to be somebody. The idea of not becoming important is seen as a lack of ambition. Maybe he did not try enough. Maybe he did not go to school. Maybe he did not have the right connections and so forth.

In today's Gospel, Jesus is on the way of becoming somebody: a great healer, a great teacher, or a great prophet. Things go wrong when he reminds his people that in the past, God had shown his favor to gentiles and not to them. They in turn come close to bringing Jesus to nothing by throwing him over the cliff. In this, Jesus prefigured how he will bring about salvation to all, by accepting God's plan for him to be brought to nothing by his own people.

We find this idea of being brought to nothing hard to take. Blessed are they who can accept and live this teaching.

PRAYER

God, our Father, each year you invite us to follow your Son anew in his journey to Jerusalem, and in his death on the Cross. Grant, we ask, that our practice of prayer, fasting, and almsgiving may enable us to be united with him in spirit during Holy Week, so that we may share with him the joy of his Resurrection on Easter. We ask this through Christ, your Son and our Lord. Amen.

GOSPEL

Peter approached Jesus and asked him, "Lord, if my brother sins against me, how often must I forgive him? As many as seven times?" Jesus answered, "I say to you, not seven times but seventy-seven times. That is why the Kingdom of heaven may be likened to a king who decided to settle accounts with his servants. When he began the accounting, a debtor was brought before him who owed him a huge amount. Since he had no way of paying it back, his master ordered him to be sold, along with his wife, his children, and all his property, in payment of the debt. At that, the servant fell down, did him homage, and said, 'Be patient with me, and I will pay you back in full.' Moved with compassion the master of that servant let him go and forgave him the loan. When that servant had left, he found one of his fellow servants who owed him a much smaller amount. He seized him and started to choke him, demanding, 'Pay back what you owe.' Falling to his knees, his fellow servant begged him, 'Be patient with me, and I will pay you back.' But he refused. Instead, he had him put in prison until he paid back the debt. Now when his fellow servants saw what had happened, they were deeply disturbed, and went to their master and reported the whole affair. His master summoned him and said to him, 'You wicked servant! I forgave you your entire debt because you begged me to. Should you not have had pity on your fellow servant, as I had pity on you?' Then in anger his master handed him over to the torturers until he should pay back the whole debt. So will my heavenly Father do to you, unless each of you forgives your brother from your heart."

MATTHEW 18: 21-35

ST. JOHN OF THE CROSS

John of the Cross writes about the spiritual outlook one must have in order to forgive. His letter is addressed to Madre María de la Encarnación.

"Do not let what is happening to me, daughter, cause you any grief, for it does not cause me any. What greatly grieves me is that the one who is not at fault is blamed. Men do not do these things, but God, who knows what is suitable for us and arranges things for our good. Think nothing else but that God ordains all, and where there is no love, put love, and you will draw out love" (L 26, July 6, 1591).

REFLECTION

When we have been attacked or had our buttons pushed, we react. We want to attack or get back at the person who hurt us. Or, if we can't do that, we may want to bide our time and seek a way of getting back.

After a while, after we have calmed down, we may want to forgive, and find it hard to do. The memory of being wronged without restitution makes it almost impossible to forgive.

John of the Cross was wronged many times; but there were two occasions when he was wronged beyond what was normal. The first time was when he was kidnapped and held captive by his friars. The second time was when he was almost driven out of the order. In each circumstance, his attitude was the same: it was not men who were doing this but God.

John of the Cross takes our basic belief that nothing happens in our lives without God permitting it and applies this belief to the all circumstances of his life, especially when he was not being loved. From this stance, he was able to forgive all who hurt him because he could see with the eyes of faith that God was using these hurts to shape the image of Christ within him. This is not to say that he found this easy or that he did not feel hurt. It is to say that with faith he was able to see through the hurts to see the hand of God at work within him arranging his soul to be more like that of Christ's. In other words, he was striving to live his life one mile below the surface where God was at work in the depths of his being. It is certainly not easy, but it is very rewarding, especially when we go before God with the image of Christ fully developed in us.

PRAYER

Lord, God, through this Season of Lent you remind us of the importance of forgiveness in imitating your Son. Grant, we ask, that we may have the grace to see all events as coming from you and thus be disposed to forgive those who harm us as your Son forgave those who harmed him. We ask this in Christ, your Son's name. Amen.

GOSPEL

JESUS SAID TO HIS DISCIPLES:

"Do not think that I have come to abolish the law or the prophets. I have come not to abolish but to fulfill. Amen, I say to you, until heaven and earth pass away, not the smallest letter or the smallest part of a letter will pass from the law, until all things have taken place. Therefore, whoever breaks one of the least of these commandments and teaches others to do so will be called least in the Kingdom of heaven. But whoever obeys and teaches these commandments will be called greatest in the Kingdom of heaven."

MATTHEW 5: 17-19

ST. JOHN OF THE CROSS

John of the Cross writes to one of his directees who was having a rough time of it. Evidently, she was in the habit of receiving lights or consolations in prayer, which had ceased. John of the Cross tells her that all she needs to do is keep the commandments and she will do fine.

"You were never better off than now because you were never so humble or so submissive, or considered yourself and all worldly things to be so small; nor did you know that you were so evil or God was so good, nor did you serve God so purely and so disinterestedly as now, nor do you follow after the imperfections of your own will and interests as perhaps you were accustomed to do. What is it you desire? What kind of life or method of procedure do you paint for yourself in this life? What do you think serving God involves other than avoiding evil, keeping his commandments, and being occupied with the things of God as best we can? When this is had, what need is there of other apprehensions or other lights and satisfactions

from this source or that? In these there is hardly ever a lack of stumbling blocks and dangers for the soul, which by its understanding and appetites is deceived and charmed; and its own faculties cause it to err. And thus God does one a great favor when he darkens the faculties and impoverishes the soul in such a way that one cannot err with these. And if one does not err in this, what need is there in order to be right other than to walk along <u>the level road of the law of God</u> and of the Church, and live only in dark and true faith and certain hope and complete charity, expecting all our blessings in heaven, living here below like pilgrims, the poor, the exiled, orphans, the thirsty, without a road and without anything, hoping for everything in heaven?" (L 19c).

REFLECTION

For centuries Christians have wondered about the place of the Law in the Old Testament in the light of the New Testament. John's Gospel says: *because while the law was given through Moses, grace and truth came through Jesus Christ* (John 1:17). However, Christians have over the centuries given more attention to God's law over the revelation of grace and truth coming from Jesus Christ.

For John of the Cross, there is no problem between Law and Grace. For him the Law serves as a guide in time of trial when God seems to be distant or not communicating through visions or locutions. Grace, on the other hand, serves as strength to weather the periods of purification.

PRAYER

Dear Lord Jesus, during your life you taught your disciples to see in you the fulfillment of the Law and the Prophets. Grant, we ask, that, as we journey with you through the Season of Lent, we too may see you as the fulfillment of the Law and the Prophets and strive to put into practice all you have taught. We ask this in your name. Amen.

GOSPEL

Jesus was driving out a demon that was mute, and when the demon had gone out, the mute man spoke and the crowds were amazed. Some of them said, "By the power of Beelzebul, the prince of demons, he drives out demons." Others, to test him, asked him for a sign from heaven. But he knew their thoughts and said to them, "Every kingdom divided against itself will be laid waste and house will fall against house. And if Satan is divided against himself, how will his kingdom stand? For you say that it is by Beelzebul that I drive out demons. If I, then, drive out demons by Beelzebul, by whom do your own people drive them out? Therefore they will be your judges. But if it is by the finger of God that I drive out demons, then the Kingdom of God has come upon you. When a strong man fully armed guards his palace, his possessions are safe. But when one stronger than he attacks and overcomes him, he takes away the armor on which he relied and distributes the spoils. Whoever is not with me is against me, and whoever does not gather with me scatters."

LUKE 11: 14-23

ST. JOHN OF THE CROSS

To those who seeking signs, John of the Cross imagines God offering these words of counsel.

"If you desire me to answer with a word of comfort, behold my Son subject to me and to others out of love for me, and afflicted, and you will see how much he answers you. If you desire me to declare some secret truths or events to you, fix your eyes only on him and you will discern hidden in him the most secret mysteries, and wisdom, and wonders of God, as my Apostle proclaims: In quo sunt omnes thesauri sapientiae et scientiae Dei absconditi *(In the Son of God are hidden all the treasures*

of the wisdom and knowledge of God) [Col 2:3]. *These treasures of wisdom and knowledge will be for you far more sublime, delightful, and advantageous than what you want to know. The Apostle, therefore, gloried, affirming that he had acted as though he knew no other than Jesus Christ and him crucified* [1 Cor 2:2]. *And if you should seek other divine or corporeal visions and revelations, behold him, become human, and you will find more than you imagine. For the Apostle also says:* In ipso habitat omnis plenitudo Divinitatis corporealiter (In Christ all the fullness of the divinity dwells bodily) [Col 2:9]" (A 2.22.6).

REFLECTION

Sooner or later everyone has to show their credentials that qualify them for the work they do. Doctors and lawyers are expected to have successfully completed graduate school. Even those who work with their hands like plumbers or pipefitters have to show signs that they are competent to do their work. In today's Gospel, Jesus is being challenged to show credentials for the work he is doing. However, he is also being accused of working hand-in-hand with the devil. Jesus is saying: if what I do is not enough for you to show you my credentials, then why are they enough for others when they perform the same healings?

Essentially, John of the Cross says the same thing: God has already shown his credentials (in case he ever needed any) in revealing his Son and standing by him in raising him from the dead. Why are these "signs" not enough for you? As always, we are challenged to live by faith in God and not in signs and wonders.

PRAYER

God, our Father, in your Son you have given us all we need to know in order to live as your adopted sons and daughters in this passing world. Grant, we ask, that we may never grow tired of gazing on him in whose image we are being transformed from day to day (see 2 Cor 3: 18) nor be distracted by those who always have new signs and wonders to report to us. We ask through Christ, our Lord. Amen.

GOSPEL

One of the scribes came to Jesus and asked him, "Which is the first of all the commandments?" Jesus replied, "The first is this: *Hear, O Israel! The Lord our God is Lord alone! You shall love the Lord your God with all your heart, with all your soul, with all your mind, and with all your strength.* The second is this: *You shall love your neighbor as yourself.* There is no other commandment greater than these." The scribe said to him, "Well said, teacher. You are right in saying, *He is One and there is no other than he.* And *to love him with all your heart, with all your understanding, with all your strength, and to love your neighbor as yourself* is worth more than all burnt offerings and sacrifices." And when Jesus saw that he answered with understanding, he said to him, "You are not far from the Kingdom of God."

And no one dared to ask him any more questions.

MARK 12: 28-34

ST. JOHN OF THE CROSS

John of the Cross writes that a soul on fire for the love of God loves God as he ought to be loved.

"One might, then, in a certain way ponder how remarkable and how strong this enkindling of love in the spirit can be. God gathers together all the strength, faculties, and appetites of the soul, spiritual and sensory alike, so the energy and power of this whole harmonious composite may be employed in this love. The soul consequently arrives at the true fulfillment of the first commandment which, neither disdaining anything human nor excluding it from this love, states: You shall love your God with your whole heart, and with your whole mind, and with your whole soul, and with all your strength [Dt 6:5]" (N 2.11.4).

John of the Cross also notes that our lack of charity toward our neighbor is often over small things.

"Lord, you return gladly and lovingly to lift up the one who offends you, but I do not turn to raise and honor the one who annoys me" (S 1.47).

REFLECTION

At the start of the spiritual life, it seems that we have to do all the work to grow and near the end it seems that God does all the work. Yet the longer we persevere in the spiritual life, the more we see that it is God who does the deeper work of ordering all our abilities to love him above all people and things; and in that love to love others as God loves them. Thus, the soul, that seeks God alone is found and loved by God alone. This in turn enables the soul to love others, even those who disappoint or contradict it, as God loves them, transforming in the love of God, loving others as God loves the soul.

PRAYER

Lord God, through this Season of Lent, you teach us to love you alone through prayer and fasting; and to love our neighbor as ourselves through almsgiving. Grant, we ask, that we may be so taken by the Holy Spirit to love you indeed with all our hearts, understanding, and strength; and to love our neighbors as we love ourselves. We ask this through Christ, our Lord. Amen.

GOSPEL

Jesus addressed this parable to those who were convinced of their own righteousness and despised everyone else. "Two people went up to the temple area to pray; one was a Pharisee and the other was a tax collector. The Pharisee took up his position and spoke this prayer to himself, 'O God, I thank you that I am not like the rest of humanity—greedy, dishonest, adulterous—or even like this tax collector. I fast twice a week, and I pay tithes on my whole income.' But the tax collector stood off at a distance and would not even raise his eyes to heaven but beat his breast and prayed, 'O God, be merciful to me a sinner.' I tell you, the latter went home justified, not the former; for everyone who exalts himself will be humbled, and the one who humbles himself will be exalted."

LUKE 18: 9-14

ST. JOHN OF THE CROSS

John of the Cross says those blessed with visions and locutions in prayer are especially susceptible to pride towards others, in the same way the Pharisee in today's Gospel is prideful toward others.

"These supernatural apprehensions of the memory, if esteemed, are also for spiritual persons a decided occasion for slipping into some presumption or vanity. Since those who do not receive these apprehensions are liberated from falling into this vice because nothing within them warrants this presumption, so, on the other hand, those who receive them will be exposed to the idea that they themselves are now important because of these supernatural communications. Although it is true that one can attribute them to God and be thankful for them and consider oneself unworthy, yet there usually remains in the spirit a certain hidden satisfaction and an esteem both for the communication and for oneself. Consequently, without one's realizing it, an abundant spiritual pride will be bred.

"This is quite evident from the displeasure and aversion these individuals feel toward anyone who does not laud their spirit or value their communications, and from the affliction they experience on thinking or being told that others receive the same favors or even better ones. All this is born of hidden self-esteem and pride. And these persons are not fully aware that they are steeped in pride. They think that a certain degree of knowledge of one's own misery is sufficient. Yet at the same time they are full of hidden self-esteem and satisfaction, more pleased with their own spirit and spiritual goods than with those of their neighbor. They resemble the pharisee who thanked God that he was not like others and that he had various virtues, and who derived self-satisfaction and presumption from the thought of these virtues [Lk 18:11–12]. Though they may not express this as the pharisee did, they habitually feel this way in their spirit. Indeed, some become so proud that they are worse than the devil. Since they observe interiorly some apprehensions and devout and sweet feelings that they think are from God, they become self-satisfied to the extent of thinking that they are very close to God and others who do not have these experiences are far beneath them and, like the pharisee, they look down upon these others" (A 3.9.1–2).

REFLECTION

Pride is one of the hardest vices to conquer. It is a habit that begins in and feeds on our self-love; and it finds ways of sticking around even when it seems that it is vanquished.

There are two remedies against this kind of pride. The first is to keep in mind what St. Teresa taught: true humility comes in knowing that all that is good (even our accomplished acts of good and virtue) comes from God; and all that is evil in us comes from ourselves. The second comes from God when and how he wills to free us from our pride through both interior and exterior suffering.

Lent is a good time to examine ourselves, to see to what extent pride still remains in us and to repent of it; and ask God to grant us whatever sufferings he sees that will free us from this vice. As a friar once told me, we are all willing to be humble; few of us are willing to be humiliated to become humble.

PRAYER

Lord, God, through this Season of Lent you call us to grow in self-knowledge as we strive to practice the disciplines of prayer, fasting, and almsgiving. Grant, we ask, that we may not fear to grow in this self-knowledge, so that we can receive the saving balm of your healing and forgiveness and thus keep us mindful of our true state before you as sinners. We ask this through Christ, our Lord. Amen.

FOURTH WEEK
OF
LENT

GOSPEL

As Jesus passed by he saw a man blind from birth. His disciples asked him, "Rabbi, who sinned, this man or his parents, that he was born blind?" Jesus answered, "Neither he nor his parents sinned; it is so that the works of God might be made visible through him. We have to do the works of the one who sent me while it is day. Night is coming when no one can work. While I am in the world, I am the light of the world." When he had said this, he spat on the ground and made clay with the saliva, and smeared the clay on his eyes, and said to him, "Go wash in the Pool of Siloam" —which means Sent. So he went and washed, and came back able to see.

His neighbors and those who had seen him earlier as a beggar said, "Isn't this the one who used to sit and beg?" Some said, "It is," but others said, "No, he just looks like him." He said, "I am." So they said to him, "How were your eyes opened?" He replied, "The man called Jesus made clay and anointed my eyes and told me, 'Go to Siloam and wash.' So I went there and washed and was able to see." And they said to him, "Where is he?" He said, "I don't know."

They brought the one who was once blind to the Pharisees. Now Jesus had made clay and opened his eyes on a sabbath. So then the Pharisees also asked him how he was able to see. He said to them, "He put clay on my eyes, and I washed, and now I can see." So some of the Pharisees said, "This man is not from God, because he does not keep the sabbath." But others said, "How can a sinful man do such signs?" And there was a division among them. So they said to the blind man again, "What do you have to say about him, since he opened your eyes?" He said, "He is a prophet."

Now the Jews did not believe that he had been blind and gained his sight until they summoned the parents of the one who had gained his sight. They asked them, "Is this your son, who you say was born blind? How does he now see?" His parents answered and said, "We know that this is our son and that he was born blind. We do not know how he sees now, nor do we know who opened his eyes. Ask him, he is of age; he can speak for himself." His parents said this because they were afraid of the Jews, for the Jews had already agreed that if anyone acknowledged him as the Christ, he would be expelled from the synagogue. For this reason his parents said, "He is of age; question him."

So a second time they called the man who had been blind and said to him, "Give God the praise! We know that this man is a sinner." He replied, "If he is a sinner, I do not know. One thing I do know is that I was blind and now I see." So they said to him, "What did he do to you? How did he open your eyes?" He answered them, "I told you already and you did not listen. Why do you want to hear it again? Do you want to become his disciples, too?" They ridiculed him and said, "You are that man's disciple; we are disciples of Moses! We know that God spoke to Moses, but we do not know where this one is from." The man answered and said to them, "This is what is so amazing, that you do not know where he is from, yet he opened my eyes. We know that God does not listen to sinners, but if one is devout and does his will, he listens to him. It is unheard of that anyone ever opened the eyes of a person born blind. If this man were not from God, he would not be able to do anything." They answered and said to him, "You were born totally in sin, and are you trying to teach us?" Then they threw him out.

When Jesus heard that they had thrown him out, he found him and said, "Do you believe in the Son of Man?" He answered and said, "Who is he, sir, that I may believe in him?" Jesus said to him, "You have seen him, the one speaking with you is he." He said, "I do believe, Lord," and he worshiped him. Then Jesus said, "I came into this world for judgment, so that those who do not see might see, and those who do see might become blind."

Some of the Pharisees who were with him heard this and said to him, "Surely we are not also blind, are we?" Jesus said to them, "If you were blind, you would have no sin; but now you are saying, 'We see,' so your sin remains."

JOHN 9: 1-41

Shorter form: JOHN 9:1, 6-9, 13-17, 34-38
Longer form may be optionally read on any day in the fourth week of Lent

ST. JOHN OF THE CROSS

John of the Cross is keen to have God take the initiative in freeing souls from their blindness to loving Him. All that God asks is that the soul rely on Him.

"In the first place it should be known that if anyone is seeking God, the Beloved is seeking that person much more. And if a soul directs to God its loving desires, which are as fragrant to him as the pillar of smoke rising from the aromatic spices of myrrh and incense [Sg 3:6], God sends it the fragrance of his ointments by which he draws it and makes it run after him [Sg 1:3], and these are his divine inspirations and touches. As often as these inspirations and touches are his, they are always bound and regulated by the perfection of his law and of faith. It is by means of this perfection that a person must always draw closer to him. Thus it should be understood that the desire for himself that God grants in all his favors of unguents and fragrant anointings is a preparation for other more precious and delicate ointments, made more according to the quality of God, until the soul is so delicately and purely prepared that it merits union with him and substantial transformation in all its faculties.

"The soul, then, should advert that God is the principal agent in this matter. He acts as guide of the blind, leading it by the hand to the place it knows not how to reach (to supernatural things of which neither its

intellect nor will nor memory can know the nature). It should use all its principal care in watching so as not to place any obstacle in the way of God, its guide on this road ordained for it by him according to the perfection of his law and of the faith, as we said" (F 3.28–29a).

REFLECTION

It is hard to imagine how blind we are at the start of the spiritual journey. Many of us begin with books on how to pray or how to meditate. Some of us take up books on journaling, or how to seek a spiritual director, or how to read a spiritual classic. It all feels like we are in control and it must seem that even God is pleased with our efforts. Then, it happens, we get caught in a great suffering from which we cannot extract ourselves. It seems like our friends and even God has abandoned us, and it all feels so hopeless. It is at this time that our real spiritual journey begins. Or, rather, it is at this time that God really initiates us into a journey that will lead us to union with him. Until God makes us as blind as the man in today's Gospel, we cannot see the light of God in his Son, Jesus. Blessed are those who can persevere through these trials. They will gain more than they have lost.

PRAYER

Lord, God, you sent us your Son so that he could be our light and make our way to you. Grant, we ask, that we may not allow ourselves to become attached to any one experience of you, so that we can be united with you in the light of faith. We ask this through Christ, our Lord. Amen.

GOSPEL

JESUS SAID TO NICODEMUS:

"Just as Moses lifted up the serpent in the desert, so must the Son of Man be lifted up, so that everyone who believes in him may have eternal life."

For God so loved the world that he gave his only Son, so that everyone who believes in him might not perish but might have eternal life. For God did not send his Son into the world to condemn the world, but that the world might be saved through him. Whoever believes in him will not be condemned, but whoever does not believe has already been condemned, because he has not believed in the name of the only Son of God. And this is the verdict, that the light came into the world, but people preferred darkness to light, because their works were evil. For everyone who does wicked things hates the light and does not come toward the light, so that his works might not be exposed. But whoever lives the truth comes to the light, so that his works may be clearly seen as done in God.

JOHN 3: 14-21

ST. JOHN OF THE CROSS

John of the Cross reminds us that God's Son came to us so we could become as children of God.

"This is what St. John meant when he said: Qui non ex sanguinibus, neque ex voluntate carnis, neque ex voluntate viri, sed ex Deo nati sunt [Jn 1:13], *which can be interpreted: He gives power for becoming the children of God (for being transformed in God) only to those who are not born of blood (combinations of the natural humors), or of the will of the flesh (the free will included in one's natural aptitude and capacity), or even less of the human will (which includes every mode and manner by which the intellect judges and understands). To none of these has he conferred the power of becoming the children of God; only to those who are born of God (those who, in their rebirth through grace and death to everything of the old self* [Eph 4:22], *rise above themselves to the supernatural and receive from God this rebirth and relationship as his children, which transcends everything imaginable).*

"St. John affirms elsewhere: Nisi quis renatus fuerit ex aqua et spiritu Sancto non potest videre regnum Dei (The one who is not reborn in the Holy Spirit will be unable to see the kingdom of God, which is the state of perfection) [Jn 3:5]. *To be reborn in the Holy Spirit during this life is to become most like God in purity, without any mixture of imperfection. Accordingly, pure transformation can be effected—although not essentially—through the participation of union"* (A 2.5.5).

REFLECTION

In primitive cultures, once a person offers a gift to another person, that other person is put in an awkward state of either accepting or declining the gift. If he declines the gift, he makes an enemy of the gift giver. If he accepts the gift, he has promised, at least implicitly, to give a gift in return. However the receiver responds, he cannot return to the situation as it was before the gift was offered him.

God did the same in giving us his Son, he gave us the gift to become his sons and daughters. As noted in the Gospel of John today, if we accept this gift, we incur an obligation to live as his sons and daughters. If we decline this gift, we make an enemy of God.

John of the Cross does not focus on the unimaginable of not accepting the offer of God's Son. Instead, he focuses on what God does in making sons and daughters out of those who accept his Son. This transformation into God by way of participation in union beats making an enemy of God by not accepting his Son. It is good news indeed.

PRAYER

Lord God, you sent forth your Son so that he could make us like you. Grant, we ask, that through the discipline of Lent, we may learn to let go of what does not lead to you and to accept in faith the new life your Son offers to us. We ask this through Christ, our Lord. Amen.

GOSPEL

Tax collectors and sinners were all drawing near to listen to Jesus, but the Pharisees and scribes began to complain, saying, "This man welcomes sinners and eats with them."

So to them Jesus addressed this parable: "A man had two sons, and the younger son said to his father, 'Father, give me the share of your estate that should come to me.' So the father divided the property between them. After a few days, the younger son collected all his belongings and set off to a distant country where he squandered his inheritance on a life of dissipation. When he had freely spent everything, a severe famine struck that country, and he found himself in dire need. So he hired himself out to one of the local citizens who sent him to his farm to tend the swine. And he longed to eat his fill of the pods on which the swine fed, but nobody gave him any. Coming to his senses he thought, 'How many of my father's hired workers have more than enough food to eat, but here am I, dying from hunger. I shall get up and go to my father and I shall say to him, "Father, I have sinned against heaven and against you. I no longer deserve to be called your son; treat me as you would treat one of your hired workers."' So he got up and went back to his father. While he was still a long way off, his father caught sight of him, and was filled with compassion. He ran to his son, embraced him and kissed him. His son said to him, 'Father, I have sinned against heaven and against you; I no longer deserve to be called your son.' But his father ordered his servants, 'Quickly, bring the finest robe and put it on him; put a ring on his finger and sandals on his feet. Take the fattened calf and slaughter it. Then let us celebrate with a feast, because this son of mine was dead, and has come to life again; he was lost, and has been found.' Then the celebration began. Now the older son had been out in the field and, on his way back, as he neared the house, he heard the sound of music and dancing. He called one of the servants and asked what this might mean. The servant said to him, 'Your brother has returned and your father has slaughtered the fattened calf because he has him back safe and sound.' He became angry, and when he refused to enter the house, his father came out and pleaded with him. He said to his father in reply, 'Look, all these years I served you and not once did I disobey your orders; yet you never gave me even a young goat to feast on with my friends. But when your son returns who swallowed up your property with prostitutes, for him you slaughter the fattened calf.' He said to him, 'My son, you are here with me always; everything I have is yours. But now we must celebrate and rejoice, because your brother was dead and has come to life again; he was lost and has been found.'"

LUKE 15: 1-3, 11-32

ST. JOHN OF THE CROSS

John of the Cross lists seven harms that come to pass by doing deeds of charity so that others see us. Two of these relate to the elder brother in today's Gospel.

"I find there are seven kinds of harm that can be incurred through vain joy in one's good works and customs; and because this harm is spiritual it is particularly ruinous.

"The first is vanity, pride, vainglory, and presumption, for one is unable to rejoice over one's works without esteeming them. This gives rise to boasting and so on, as is said of the pharisee in the Gospel: He prayed and sought friendship with God by boasting of his fasting and performance of other good works [Lk 18:11–12].

"The second is usually linked with the first. It is that people make comparisons judging others to be evil and imperfect, supposing that the deeds and works of others are not as good as their own. Interiorly they have less regard for others, and they sometimes manifest this exteriorly in word. The pharisee also had this defect since he said in his prayer: I give you thanks that I am not like other men: robbers, unjust, and adulterers [Lk 18:11]. *Through one act he incurred the two kinds of harm: self-esteem and contempt for others.*

"Many today also do so when they boast: 'I am not like so and so, nor do I do anything similar to what this or that one does.' Many are even worse than the pharisee. Though the pharisee not only bore contempt for others in general, but even indicated a particular individual in declaring, I am not like this publican [Lk 18:11], *many persons, content with neither of these two attitudes, even become angry and envious in noticing that others receive praise or accomplish more or have greater value than they themselves"* (A 3.28.1–3).

REFLECTION

The older son in today's Gospel took secret pride in his good behavior as opposed to the wayward behavior of his younger brother. He thought for sure that if his father were to reward anybody, he would reward him. Like the pharisee, the elder brother could have said, "I am not like my younger brother!" As is common in the Gospel of Luke, the tables are turned. It is not those who keep the Law who are rewarded but those who repent of their sinfulness that get the better cuts of meat and so forth.

Many of us reading this Gospel only get part of message right: not to compare ourselves with others who seem less Christian than we are. John of the Cross goes a little further, we need to grow in the self-knowledge of our pride and desire for God to see us as better than others. When we do, we can see that we, too, need to travel the road of repentance that the younger brother made and be reconciled with God. Then we, too, will be invited to the dinner table of all those reconciled with God.

PRAYER

Lord, God, through the Season of Lent, you teach us how to be your servants in a true spirit of gratitude and love. Grant, we ask, that in our service we may take our greatest joy in the fact that you have called us to be your Son's partners in the work of salvation. We ask this in the name of Christ, your Son. Amen.

GOSPEL

At that time Jesus left [Samaria] for Galilee. For Jesus himself testified that a prophet has no honor in his native place. When he came into Galilee, the Galileans welcomed him, since they had seen all he had done in Jerusalem at the feast; for they themselves had gone to the feast.

Then he returned to Cana in Galilee, where he had made the water wine. Now there was a royal official whose son was ill in Capernaum. When he heard that Jesus had arrived in Galilee from Judea, he went to him and asked him to come down and heal his son, who was near death. Jesus said to him, "Unless you people see signs and wonders, you will not believe." The royal official said to him, "Sir, come down before my child dies." Jesus said to him, "You may go; your son will live." The man believed what Jesus said to him and left. While the man was on his way back, his slaves met him and told him that his boy would live. He asked them when he began to recover. They told him, "The fever left him yesterday, about one in the afternoon." The father realized that just at that time Jesus had said to him, "Your son will live," and he and his whole household came to believe. Now this was the second sign Jesus did when he came to Galilee from Judea.

JOHN 4: 43-54

ST. JOHN OF THE CROSS

John of the Cross might have counseled the royal official thusly:

"You do very well, O soul, to seek him ever as one hidden, for you exalt God and approach very near him when you consider him higher and deeper than anything you can reach. Hence pay no attention, neither partially nor entirely, to anything your faculties can grasp. I mean that you should never seek satisfaction in what you understand about God, but in what you do not understand about him. Never pause to love and delight in your understanding and experience of God, but love and delight in what you cannot understand or experience of him. Such is the way, as we said, of seeking him in faith. However surely it may seem that you find, experience, and understand God, because he is inaccessible and concealed you must always regard him as hidden, and serve him who is hidden in a secret way. Do not be like the many foolish ones who, in their lowly understanding of God, think that when they do not understand, taste, or experience him, he is far away and utterly concealed. The contrary belief would be truer. The less distinct is their understanding of him, the closer they approach him, since in the words of the prophet David, he made darkness his hiding place [Ps 18:11]. *Thus in drawing near him you will experience darkness because of the weakness of your eye"* (C 1.12).

REFLECTION

The royal official in today's Gospel came to Jesus to ask for a favor for his child before he died. Jesus tested the man's faith to see if he truly believed or if he was going to believe only on account of a sign. Behind the rebuff on Jesus' part, there was also an invitation for the royal official to develop a deeper relationship with Jesus based on faith.

John of the Cross has in mind every Christian who lives by faith in Jesus rather than in seeking signs and wonders. The deeper the faith the more one can live in God's presence. The less we depend on what we can understand about God from our thoughts or experience about

God, the more we can know him as he is. As John of the Cross said in his Second Book of the Ascent:

"For the likeness between faith and God is so close that no other differ-ence exists than that between believing in God and seeing him. Just as God is infinite, faith proposes him to us as infinite. Just as there are three Persons in one God, it presents him to us in this way. And just as God is darkness to our intellect, so faith dazzles and blinds us. Only by means of faith, in divine light exceeding all understanding, does God manifest himself to the soul. The greater one's faith the closer is one's union with God" (A 2.9.1).

Since faith does lead us to a deeper relationship with God, then it behooves us, who believe in Jesus as the Son of God, to practice this virtue of faith through prayer, fasting, and almsgiving as we near the end of Lent.

PRAYER

Lord, God, through the discipline of Lent you call us to a deeper faith in your Son through fasting, prayer, and almsgiving. Grant, we ask, that we may profit from this opportunity to grow in faith, so that when trials come, we may learn of your Son through faith and not to look for signs. We ask this through Christ, our Lord. Amen.

GOSPEL

There was a feast of the Jews, and Jesus went up to Jerusalem. Now there is in Jerusalem at the Sheep Gate a pool called in Hebrew Bethesda, with five porticoes. In these lay a large number of ill, blind, lame, and crippled. One man was there who had been ill for thirty-eight years. When Jesus saw him lying there and knew that he had been ill for a long time, he said to him, "Do you want to be well?" The sick man answered him, "Sir, I have no one to put me into the pool when the water is stirred up; while I am on my way, someone else gets down there before me." Jesus said to him, "Rise, take up your mat, and walk." Immediately the man became well, took up his mat, and walked.

Now that day was a sabbath. So the Jews said to the man who was cured, "It is the sabbath, and it is not lawful for you to carry your mat." He answered them, "The man who made me well told me, 'Take up your mat and walk.'" They asked him, "Who is the man who told you, 'Take it up and walk'?" The man who was healed did not know who it was, for Jesus had slipped away, since there was a crowd there. After this Jesus found him in the temple area and said to him, "Look, you are well; do not sin any more, so that nothing worse may happen to you." The man went and told the Jews that Jesus was the one who had made him well. Therefore, the Jews began to persecute Jesus because he did this on a sabbath.

JOHN 5: 1-16

ST. JOHN OF THE CROSS

As we turn now from following Christ as healer and teacher to Christ persecuted for our redemption, St. John of the Cross offers this teaching for those whom God has called to follow his Son when he felt alone and abandoned by his friends.

"Such persons also feel forsaken and despised by creatures, particularly by their friends. David immediately adds: You have withdrawn my friends and acquaintances far from me; they have considered me an abomination [Ps. 88:8]. *Jonah, as one who also underwent this experience, both physically and spiritually in the belly of the whale, testifies:* You have cast me out into the deep, into the heart of the sea, and the current surrounded me; all its whirlpools and waves passed over me and I said: I am cast from the sight of your eyes; yet I shall see your holy temple again *(he says this because God purifies the soul that it might see his temple);* the waters encircled me even to the soul, the abyss went round about me, the open sea covered my head, I descended to the lowest parts of the mountains, the locks of the earth closed me up forever [Jon. 2:4–7]. *The 'locks' refer to the soul's imperfections that hinder it from enjoying the delights of this contemplation"* (N 2.6.3).

REFLECTION

The man whom Jesus cured was not one of his friends; but he did point out Jesus as the man who cured him and this lead to his being persecuted because he cured on the Sabbath. However it comes about, persecution from one's own is harder than persecution from strangers. It is not that they can hurt us any less physically, but rather our own know us from the inside and so can hurt us in the more intimate areas of our being. As the psalmist said:

"If an enemy had reviled me, that I could bear; If my foe had viewed me with contempt, from that I could hide. But it was you, my other self, my comrade and friend, You, whose company I enjoyed, at whose side I walked in procession in the house of God" (Ps 55:13–15).

This is why John of the Cross mentions this experience as a prelude to the dark night of the soul. Whereas the previous sufferings were in a certain sense consoling, the ones of the dark night are more disconcerting because it feels like God has abandoned us along with everyone else. Even though we know by faith that this is not true, our faith does not give us the affective assurance that it used to give us. That is why we need to frequently exercise our faith in good times and in the liturgical seasons so that when the seasons of rejection come, our faith will be there to see us through.

PRAYER

Lord God, through the Season of Lent, you call us to follow your Son through a life of prayer, fasting, and almsgiving. Grant, we ask, as we now follow your Son persecuted, that we may embrace our crosses with faith, hope, and charity in imitation of him who became afflicted, so that we may share life with You. We ask this in his name. Amen.

GOSPEL

Jesus answered the Jews: "My Father is at work until now, so I am at work." For this reason they tried all the more to kill him, because he not only broke the sabbath but he also called God his own father, making himself equal to God.

Jesus answered and said to them, "Amen, amen, I say to you, the Son cannot do anything on his own, but only what he sees the Father doing; for what he does, the Son will do also. For the Father loves the Son and shows him everything that he himself does, and he will show him greater works than these, so that you may be amazed. For just as the Father raises the dead and gives life, so also does the Son give life to whomever he wishes. Nor does the Father judge anyone, but he has given all judgment to the Son, so that all may honor the Son just as they honor the Father. Whoever does not honor the Son does not honor the Father who sent him. Amen, amen, I say to you, whoever hears my word and believes in the one who sent me has eternal life and will not come to condemnation, but has passed from death to life. Amen, amen, I say to you, the hour is coming and is now here when the dead will hear the voice of the Son of God, and those who hear will live. For just as the Father has life in himself, so also he gave to the Son the possession of life in himself. And he gave him power to exercise judgment, because he is the Son of Man. Do not be amazed at this, because the hour is coming in which all who are in the tombs will hear his voice and will come out, those who have done good deeds to the resurrection of life, but those who have done wicked deeds to the resurrection of condemnation.

"I cannot do anything on my own; I judge as I hear, and my judgment is just, because I do not seek my own will but the will of the one who sent me."

JOHN 5: 17-30

ST. JOHN OF THE CROSS

John of the Cross has much to say about the relationship between the Son of God and the Father as well as the relationship of the soul to the Son of God and the Father.

"No knowledge or power can describe how this happens, unless by explaining how the Son of God attained and merited such a high state for us, the power to be children of God, as St. John says [Jn 1:12]. *Thus the Son asked of the Father in St. John's Gospel:* Father, I desire that where I am those you have given me may also be with me, that they may see the glory you have given me [Jn. 17:24], *that is, that they may perform in us by participation the same work that I do by nature; that is, breathe the Holy Spirit. And he adds:* I do not ask, Father, only for those present, but for those also who will believe in me through their doctrine; that all of them may be one as you, Father, in me and I in you, that thus they be one in us. The glory which you have given me I have given them that they may be one as we are one, I in them and you in me; that they may be perfect in one; that the world may know that you have sent me and loved them as you have loved me [Jn 17:20–23]. *The Father loves them by communicating to them the same love he communicates to the Son, though not naturally as to the Son but, as we said, through unity and transformation of love. It should not be thought that the Son desires here to ask the Father that the saints be one with him essentially and naturally as the Son is with the Father, but that they may be so through the union of love, just as the Father and the Son are one in unity of love"* (C 39.5).

REFLECTION

Jesus in today's Gospel speaks of his relationship with the Father. It is a mysterious relationship because it is known only to the Father and him alone. Jesus tries to explain to his people that what he has done, and what he continues to do, is based on his relationship with the Father. As he said: *My Father is at work until now, so I am at work.* He also explains how he and the Father are related: *For the Father loves the Son and shows him everything that he himself does, and he will show him greater works than these, so that you may be amazed.*

John of the Cross also writes about the inner life between Jesus and his Father; however, he does so in order to explain how the Christian, who has been initiated into this life by God, lives in this atmosphere of love that takes place between the Father and the Son.

The life of faith written about earlier is difficult because it has so little to do with our own habitual way of understanding life. This is because God is not one object along with all other objects; or one creature along with all the other creatures, he is the Source and Lord of them all. Still, for those who persevere in the life of faith and accept God's invitation to fellowship with him through his Son and on his own terms, God opens up a new life for them, a life in which the Father and the Son are in communion with one another.

PRAYER

Dear Lord Jesus, through your Incarnation you merited for those who believe in you to become children of God; and through your Passion and death you brought about their reconciliation with God the Father. Grant, we ask, that, as we continue to travel with you through the remainder of the Season of Lent and into the period of your Passion and death, we may grow to be more selfless by participating in your spirit. We ask this in your name. Amen.

GOSPEL

JESUS SAID TO THE JEWS:

"If I testify on my own behalf, my testimony is not true. But there is another who testifies on my behalf, and I know that the testimony he gives on my behalf is true. You sent emissaries to John, and he testified to the truth. I do not accept human testimony, but I say this so that you may be saved. He was a burning and shining lamp, and for a while you were content to rejoice in his light. But I have testimony greater than John's. The works that the Father gave me to accomplish, these works that I perform testify on my behalf that the Father has sent me. Moreover, the Father who sent me has testified on my behalf. But you have never heard his voice nor seen his form, and you do not have his word remaining in you, because you do not believe in the one whom he has sent. You search the Scriptures, because you think you have eternal life through them; even they testify on my behalf. But you do not want to come to me to have life.

"I do not accept human praise; moreover, I know that you do not have the love of God in you. I came in the name of my Father, but you do not accept me; yet if another comes in his own name, you will accept him. How can you believe, when you accept praise from one another and do not seek the praise that comes from the only God? Do not think that I will accuse you before the Father: the one who will accuse you is Moses, in whom you have placed your hope. For if you had believed Moses, you would have believed me, because he wrote about me. But if you do not believe his writings, how will you believe my words?"

JOHN 5: 31-47

ST. JOHN OF THE CROSS

This is the way Christians should do good works and seek eternal life.

"Thus, through their good customs and virtues they should fix their eyes only on the service and honor of God. Without this aspect the virtues are worth nothing in God's sight. This is evident in the Gospel in the case of the ten virgins. They had all preserved their virginity and done good works, yet because five of them had not rejoiced in this second way (by directing their joy in these works to God), but rather in the first, rejoicing vainly in the possession of these works, they were rejected from heaven and left without any gratitude or reward from their spouse [Mt 25:1–13]. Also many of the ancients possessed numerous virtues and engaged in good works, and many Christians have them today and accomplish wonderful deeds; but such works are of no profit for eternal life because of failure to seek only the honor and glory of God.

"Christians, then, should rejoice not if they accomplish good works and abide by good customs, but if they do these things out of love for God alone, without any other motive. As those who work only for the service of God will receive a more elevated reward of glory, so those who work for other motives will suffer greater shame when they stand before God.

"For the sake of directing their joy in moral goods to God, Christians should keep in mind that the value of their good works, fasts, alms, penances, and so on, is not based on quantity and quality so much as on the love of God practiced in them; and consequently that these works are of greater excellence in the measure both that the love of God by which they are performed is more pure and entire and that self-interest diminishes with respect to pleasure, comfort, praise, and earthly or heavenly joy. They should not set their heart on the pleasure, comfort, savor, and other elements of self-interest these good works and practices usually entail, but recollect their joy in God and desire to serve him through these means. And through purgation and darkness as to this joy in moral goods they should

desire in secret that only God be pleased and joyful over their works. They should have no other interest or satisfaction than the honor and glory of God. Thus all the strength of their will in regard to these moral goods will be recollected in God" (A 3.27.4b–5).

REFLECTION

Throughout this part of John's Gospel, Jesus is at pains to explain that he does the works he does because of his relationship with the Father. As he sees the Father do, so he does in return. He did not do them so that he would be praised but rather that the Father would be believed in and loved.

John of the Cross has the same end in view for Christians in the works they perform. They should not perform them to take satisfaction in them or to have God's approval for doing them but for God alone.

For John of the Cross, it is not the amount of work that we do for God that counts, but the spirit in which we do them, the spirit of not seeking joy for ourselves alone but finding joy in God alone. The more we do this inflamed with the love of God and for God, the more God's love will enter into them and take them into his Spirit, and share in the life of the Son.

PRAYER

Lord God, you sent your Son so that all who believe in him may have eternal life. Grant, we ask, that, as we follow him through the remainder of Lent, we may perform our works of prayer, fasting, and almsgiving for your glory and not for our imagined approval from you. We ask this through Christ, your Son. Amen.

GOSPEL

Jesus moved about within Galilee; he did not wish to travel in Judea, because the Jews were trying to kill him. But the Jewish feast of Tabernacles was near.

But when his brothers had gone up to the feast, he himself also went up, not openly but as it were in secret.

Some of the inhabitants of Jerusalem said, "Is he not the one they are trying to kill? And look, he is speaking openly and they say nothing to him. Could the authorities have realized that he is the Christ? But we know where he is from. When the Christ comes, no one will know where he is from." So Jesus cried out in the temple area as he was teaching and said, "You know me and also know where I am from. Yet I did not come on my own, but the one who sent me, whom you do not know, is true. I know him, because I am from him, and he sent me." So they tried to arrest him, but no one laid a hand upon him, because his hour had not yet come.

JOHN 7: 1-2, 10, 25-30

ST. JOHN OF THE CROSS

In these counsels, John of the Cross gives directives on how to imitate Christ, who suffered persecution for us.

"Though these counsels for the conquering of the appetites are brief and few in number, I believe they are as profitable and efficacious as they are concise. A person who sincerely wants to practice them will need no others since all the others are included in these.

"First, have habitual desire to imitate Christ in all your deeds by bringing your life into conformity with his. You must then study his life in

order to know how to imitate him and behave in all events as he would.

"*Second, in order to be successful in this imitation, renounce and remain empty of any sensory satisfaction that is not purely for the honor and glory of God. Do this out of love for Jesus Christ. In his life he had no other gratification, nor desired any other, than the fulfillment of his Father's will, which he called his meat and food* [Jn 4:34].

"*For example, if you are offered the satisfaction of hearing things that have no relation to the service and glory of God, do not desire this pleasure or the hearing of these things. When you have an opportunity for the gratification of looking upon objects that will not help you love God more, do not desire this gratification or sight. And if in speaking there is a similar opportunity, act in the same way. And so on with all the senses insofar as you can duly avoid such satisfaction. If you cannot escape the experience of this satisfaction, it will be sufficient to have no desire for it.*

"*By this method you should endeavor, then, to leave the senses as though in darkness, mortified and empty of that satisfaction. With such vigilance you will gain a great deal in a short time*" (A 1.13.2–4).

REFLECTION

As we come to the end of the Fourth Week of Lent, we see that Jesus is becoming more and more persecuted. He has to hide more and move about in secret. John of the Cross gives Christians advice on how they are to imitate Jesus during this period in which he is being persecuted.

The first thing he recommends is that we must study and imitate the life of Jesus. Reading the daily readings and praying over them is the best way to study the life of Jesus. Through the liturgical year of readings, the Church follows her spouse Jesus and strives to understand him more and more. An example of this is the icon of Our Lady of Mount Carmel. She wears blue but her son wears red. The more she looks upon him, the wider her eyes grow, and the smaller her ears and mouth grow. Even the periphery of her clothing is taking on a shade of red. She is thus transformed into her son by studying him closely and accepting the destiny of his passion in the color red.

The second thing he tells us to do is to do what our state of life requires of us with a deep love for God and not for our personal gratification. We live in a world where we are told that unless we are stimulated and find our joy in being stimulated we will be nothing. To be in our world is to be stimulated and to enjoy being stimulated; but for John of the Cross this is to become more and more removed from our deepest center where God abides. To find God, we must find ways to be free from incessant stimulation.

The more we study the life of Jesus either through the readings of the liturgical year or in our own personal study; and the more we strive to limit the impact of commercials upon us by not seeking any pleasure in what we see or hear in them, the more we open ourselves up for God and encounter him in our deepest center where he resides.

PRAYER

Lord Jesus, you testified to the Father even though it meant conflict, persecution, and rejection for you. Grant, we ask, that we may study your life more closely, renounce all that is contrary to your teaching, and to do all for the glory of God, the Father, as you did. We ask this in your name. Amen.

GOSPEL

Some in the crowd who heard these words of Jesus said, "This is truly the Prophet." Others said, "This is the Christ." But others said, "The Christ will not come from Galilee, will he? Does not Scripture say that the Christ will be of David's family and come from Bethlehem, the village where David lived?" So a division occurred in the crowd because of him. Some of them even wanted to arrest him, but no one laid hands on him.

So the guards went to the chief priests and Pharisees, who asked them, "Why did you not bring him?" The guards answered, "Never before has anyone spoken like this man." So the Pharisees answered them, "Have you also been deceived? Have any of the authorities or the Pharisees believed in him? But this crowd, which does not know the law, is accursed." Nicodemus, one of their members who had come to him earlier, said to them, "Does our law condemn a man before it first hears him and finds out what he is doing?" They answered and said to him, "You are not from Galilee also, are you? Look and see that no prophet arises from Galilee."

Then each went to his own house.

JOHN 7: 40-53

ST. JOHN OF THE CROSS

John of the Cross advises us on how to approach sufferings.

"People, then, should live with great patience and constancy in all the tribulations and trials God places on them, whether they be exterior or interior, spiritual or bodily, great or small, and they should accept them all as from God's hand as a good remedy and not flee from them, for they bring health. In this matter let them take the counsel of the Wise Man:

If the spirit of him who has power descends upon you, do not abandon your place *(the place and site of your probation, which is the trial he sends you),* for the cure will make great sins cease [Eccl. 10:4]; *that is, it will cut of the roots of your sins and imperfections—your evil habits. The combat of trials, distress, and temptations deadens the evil and imperfect habits of the soul and purifies and strengthens it. People should hold in esteem the interior and exterior trials God sends them, realizing that there are few who merit to be brought to perfection through suffering and to undergo trials for the sake of so high a state"* (F 2.30).

REFLECTION

No one likes suffering. Our age has become quite adept at making suffering not only more tolerable but finding ways to avoid suffering altogether. This is not to say we should not be mindful of our health, taking medicine, or seeing a doctor; but it must be asked: in the end, after all our efforts to avoid pain, have we not closed the door to encountering God? Have we not in some way short-circuited the way God has planned for us to encounter him? Is this not why people have become addicted to drugs? And the pain that they have sought to avoid has instead wrought a deeper and more painful suffering without hope? There are no simple answers to these questions, but they need to be asked because upon our answer lies the openness to encounter God through them or not.

Neither Jesus, nor John of the Cross knew the strength of our age to keep us from suffering; but they did offer hope, to those who listened to them, that the acceptance of suffering for the love of God does open us up to encountering God more deeply. As John of the Cross describes this benefit of encountering God through suffering:

"The soul knows in this state that everything has ended well and that now ("As is its darkness, so is its light." [Ps. 139:12]), and that, as it was a sharer of tribulations, it is now a sharer of consolations and of the kingdom [2 Cor 1:7]. For God repays the interior and exterior trials very

well with divine goods for the soul and body, so there is not a trial that does not have a corresponding and considerable reward. It proclaims this by saying with full satisfaction: 'and pays every debt.' It thanks God in this verse for having withdrawn it from trials, as David also did in his psalm: What great tribulations you have shown me, many and difficult, and you have freed me from them all, and have brought me back again from the abyss of the earth. You have multiplied your magnificence and turning to me you have comforted me [Ps 71:20–21]" (F 2.31).

For John of the Cross, God pays back every debt from suffering. God is a grateful lover to those who suffer out of love for him.

PRAYER

God, our Father, as we come to the end of the Fourth Week of Lent and enter the Fifth Week, we see your Son become more and more despised and rejected. Grant, we ask, that we may not let our need for recognition and esteem keep us from following your Son, but that our desire to follow him will enable us to "live with great patience and constancy in all the tribulations and trials" you place upon us. We ask this in Jesus, your Son's name. Amen.

FIFTH WEEK
OF
LENT

GOSPEL

Now a man was ill, Lazarus from Bethany, the village of Mary and her sister Martha. Mary was the one who had anointed the Lord with perfumed oil and dried his feet with her hair; it was her brother Lazarus who was ill. So the sisters sent word to Jesus saying, "Master, the one you love is ill." When Jesus heard this he said, "This illness is not to end in death, but is for the glory of God, that the Son of God may be glorified through it." Now Jesus loved Martha and her sister and Lazarus. So when he heard that he was ill, he remained for two days in the place where he was. Then after this he said to his disciples, "Let us go back to Judea." The disciples said to him, "Rabbi, the Jews were just trying to stone you, and you want to go back there?" Jesus answered, "Are there not twelve hours in a day? If one walks during the day, he does not stumble, because he sees the light of this world. But if one walks at night, he stumbles, because the light is not in him." He said this, and then told them, "Our friend Lazarus is asleep, but I am going to awaken him." So the disciples said to him, "Master, if he is asleep, he will be saved." But Jesus was talking about his death, while they thought that he meant ordinary sleep. So then Jesus said to them clearly, "Lazarus has died. And I am glad for you that I was not there, that you may believe. Let us go to him." So Thomas, called Didymus, said to his fellow disciples, "Let us also go to die with him."

When Jesus arrived, he found that Lazarus had already been in the tomb for four days. Now Bethany was near Jerusalem, only about two miles away. And many of the Jews had come to Martha and Mary to comfort them about their brother. When Martha heard that Jesus was coming, she went to meet him; but Mary sat at home. Martha said to Jesus, "Lord, if you had been here, my brother would not have died. But even now I know that whatever you ask of God, God will give you." Jesus said to her, "Your brother will rise." Martha said to him, "I know he will rise, in the resurrection on the last day." Jesus told her, "I am the resurrection and the life; whoever believes in me, even if he dies, will live, and everyone who lives and believes in me will never die. Do you believe this?" She said to him, "Yes, Lord. I have come to believe that you are the Christ, the Son of God, the one who is coming into the world."

When she had said this, she went and called her sister Mary secretly, saying, "The teacher is here and is asking for you." As soon as she heard this, she rose quickly and went to him. For Jesus had not yet come into the village, but was still where Martha had met him. So when the Jews who were with her in the house comforting her saw Mary get up quickly and go out, they followed her, presuming that she was going to the tomb to weep there. When Mary came to where Jesus was and saw him, she fell at his feet and said to him, "Lord, if you had been here, my brother would not have died." When Jesus saw her weeping and the Jews who had come with her weeping, he became perturbed and deeply troubled, and said, "Where have you laid him?" They said to him, "Sir, come and see." And Jesus wept. So the Jews said, "See how he loved him." But some of them said, "Could not the one who opened the eyes of the blind man have done something so that this man would not have died?"

So Jesus, perturbed again, came to the tomb. It was a cave, and a stone lay across it. Jesus said, "Take away the stone." Martha, the dead man's sister, said to him, "Lord, by now there will be a stench; he has been dead for four days." Jesus said to her, "Did I not tell you that if you believe you will see the glory of God?" So they took away the stone. And Jesus raised his eyes and said, "Father, I thank you for hearing me. I know that you always hear me; but because of the crowd here I have said this, that they may believe that you sent me." And when he had said this, he cried out in a loud voice, "Lazarus, come out!" The dead man came out, tied hand and foot with burial bands, and his face was wrapped in a cloth. So Jesus said to them, "Untie him and let him go."

Now many of the Jews who had come to Mary and seen what he had done began to believe in him.

JOHN 11: 1-45

Shorter form: JOHN 11:3-7, 17, 20-27, 33b-45
Longer form may be optionally read on any day in the fifth week of Lent

ST. JOHN OF THE CROSS

John of the Cross explains how Christians should pray when they are lacking something.

"It should be pointed out that in this verse the soul does no more than disclose to the Beloved her need and suffering. The discreet lover does not care to ask for what she lacks and desires, but only indicates this need so the Beloved may do what he pleases. When the Blessed Virgin spoke to her beloved Son at the wedding feast at Cana in Galilee, she did not ask directly for the wine, but merely remarked: They have no wine [Jn 2:3]. *And the sisters of Lazarus did not send to ask our Lord to cure their brother, but to tell him that Lazarus whom he loved was sick [Jn 11:3]. There are three reasons for this: First, the Lord knows what is suitable for us better than we do; second, the Beloved has more compassion when he beholds the need and resignation of a soul that loves him; third, the soul is better safeguarded against self-love and possessiveness by indicating its lack, rather than asking for what in its opinion is wanting. The soul, now, does likewise by just indicating her three needs. Her words are similar to saying:* Tell my Beloved, since I am sick and he alone is my health, to give me health; and, since I suffer and he alone is my joy, to give me joy; and, since I die and he alone is my life, to give me life" (C 2.8).

REFLECTION

From childhood on, we learn that prayer is for something we need or want. For example, if we are feeling sick, we pray for the return to health. If we are without a job, we pray that we will find one soon. If we are lonely, we pray for a friend or a spouse and so forth. Clearly, we pray for what we need.

John of the Cross proposes another way of praying. Instead of praying for what we need or what we want, he writes that we should present our needs to God as what we are lacking. So instead of praying for a job, we should tell our Lord: "Lord, I do not have a job." Or, if it is something else that we feel is painfully lacking in our life, we should tell our Lord: "Lord, it is such and so that I am lacking." For John of the Cross, this gives us the freedom to receive from God what God wants to give us with open hands. John of the Cross is very keen that, even in prayer, we seek not so much ourselves, but God and his will for us. As far as he is concerned, the more we seek God, and his will for us, the more God will be able to give us what we need and more, himself. For John of the Cross, there is no greater gift God can give than God himself. All other gifts, no matter how important they might feel at the present moment, pale in comparison to the intimate love that God wants us to have with himself through his Son and in the Holy Spirit.

To bolster this way of praying, John of the Cross cites the way Mary petitioned her Son at Cana; and the way the sisters of Lazarus let Jesus know that their brother was sick. This way of petitioning our Lord may be a little difficult at first because we are more used to the earlier way of praying when we stated what we wanted or needed. The advantage of using John of the Cross' way is that it protects us from self-love and self-seeking; and it orients us to seek God first and his way. If this sounds too ungratifying, it is. It is what John of the Cross holds out to us as the surer way of completing our Lenten journey (and the journey of our life) in finding Christ risen from the dead. If you need any more persuasion, recall what our Lord said: *"But seek first the kingdom (of God) and his righteousness, and all these things will be given you besides"* (Mt 6:33).

PRAYER

Lord God, when Mary, the mother of your Son, saw the lack of wine at the wedding, she told her Son "they have no wine" and when the sisters of Lazarus saw their brother lacking health, they sent word to your Son to let him know it. Grant, we ask, that we may have the humility to pray as they did, so that we may grow in trust in you, knowing what is suitable for us, we present ourselves resigned to your will and thus grow to love you more than ourselves. We ask this in Jesus, your Son's name. Amen.

GOSPEL

Some Greeks who had come to worship at the Passover Feast came to Philip, who was from Bethsaida in Galilee, and asked him, "Sir, we would like to see Jesus." Philip went and told Andrew; then Andrew and Philip went and told Jesus. Jesus answered them, "The hour has come for the Son of Man to be glorified. Amen, amen, I say to you, unless a grain of wheat falls to the ground and dies, it remains just a grain of wheat; but if it dies, it produces much fruit. Whoever loves his life loses it, and whoever hates his life in this world will preserve it for eternal life. Whoever serves me must follow me, and where I am, there also will my servant be. The Father will honor whoever serves me.

"I am troubled now. Yet what should I say? 'Father, save me from this hour'? But it was for this purpose that I came to this hour. Father, glorify your name." Then a voice came from heaven, "I have glorified it and will glorify it again." The crowd there heard it and said it was thunder; but others said, "An angel has spoken to him." Jesus answered and said, "This voice did not come for my sake but for yours. Now is the time of judgement on this world; now the ruler of this world will be driven out. And when I am lifted up from the earth, I will draw everyone to myself." He said this indicating the kind of death he would die.

JOHN 12: 20-33

ST. JOHN OF THE CROSS

John of the Cross explains of what a true locution from God consists.

"St. John says that while the Lord Jesus was praying to his Father in the conflict and anguish occasioned by his enemies, an inner voice came to him from heaven and comforted him in his humanity. The sound of this voice, which the Jews heard as though coming from outside, was so deep and loud that some said it had thundered and others that an angel from heaven had spoken [Jn 12:27–29]. The reason is that the voice, which was heard as though coming from without, denoted and manifested the fortitude and strength that was interiorly bestowed on Christ in his humanity.

"It must not be thought on this account that the soul fails to receive in its spirit the sound of the spiritual voice. It should be noted that the spiritual voice is the effect produced in the spirit, just as the sound in the ear and knowledge in the spirit are effects of the material voice. David meant this when he said: Ecce dabit voci suae vocem virtutis (Behold that God will give to his voice the voice of power) [Ps 68:33]. This power is the interior voice, because when David said he will give to his voice the voice of power, he meant that to the exterior voice, heard from without, he will give the voice of power that is heard from within.

"Hence it should be known that God is an infinite voice, and by communicating himself to the soul in this way he produces the effect of an immense voice" (C 14 & 15.10c–e).

REFLECTION

One phenomenon that people often experience as they grow in prayer is what some spiritual writers call locutions. For example, a person is at prayer, and he senses that God is saying to him, "I will help you." or "Do not be afraid." and so forth. Sometimes these locutions can be quite long. The question that arises is: What to make of them? John of the Cross believes that it is better to make nothing of them rather than something because there is less risk if we take the former path rather than the latter. With the latter, we may confuse our own desires with those of God. And even when these locutions are of God, we do God no offense by not putting any stock in them but instead believing in him by faith. John of the Cross does see one exception to this rule and that is when God actually speaks to the soul. When he does, he is very brief and he immediately effects what he is saying in the soul. At that point, the soul need not wonder whether the locution is from God or not. The effect of God's message has already taken place in him.

PRAYER

God our Father, in times past you spoke in partial and various ways to our ancestors through the prophets; and in these last days, you spoke to us through your Son, whom you made heir of all things and through whom you created the universe, who is the refulgence of your glory, the very imprint of your being, and who sustains all things by your mighty word (see Hebrews 1:1–3). Grant, we ask, that we may not get lost in the fearful prophecies of the future, but rather look to your Son as your final word for our future. We ask this through Christ, Our Lord. Amen.

GOSPEL

Jesus went to the Mount of Olives. But early in the morning he arrived again in the temple area, and all the people started coming to him, and he sat down and taught them. Then the scribes and the Pharisees brought a woman who had been caught in adultery and made her stand in the middle. They said to him, "Teacher, this woman was caught in the very act of committing adultery. Now in the law, Moses commanded us to stone such women. So what do you say?" They said this to test him, so that they could have some charge to bring against him. Jesus bent down and began to write on the ground with his finger. But when they continued asking him, he straightened up and said to them, "Let the one among you who is without sin be the first to throw a stone at her." Again he bent down and wrote on the ground. And in response, they went away one by one, beginning with the elders. So he was left alone with the woman before him. Then Jesus straightened up and said to her, "Woman, where are they? Has no one condemned you?" She replied, "No one, sir." Then Jesus said, "Neither do I condemn you. Go, and from now on do not sin any more."

JOHN 8: 1-11

ST. JOHN OF THE CROSS

John of the Cross writes at great length about what souls suffer when the light of God's love shines upon them and reveals their sinfulness. It was the state of this poor woman caught in adultery. However, as Jesus was merciful to her, so is God merciful to the soul.

"Remembering here all these mercies and aware that she has been placed with so much dignity close to the Bridegroom, she rejoices immeasurably in the delight of thanksgiving and love. The memory of that former state, so unsightly and abject, notably promotes this gratitude and love. She was not only unprepared for and unworthy of God's gaze, but she did not even deserve that he pronounce her name, as he says through David [Ps 16:4]. Conscious that in herself there is no reason, or possibility of a reason, why God should look at and exalt her, but that this reason is only in God, in his mere will and beautiful grace, she ascribes her misery to herself, and all her good possessions to the Beloved. Aware that through them she now merits what previously she did not, she takes courage and becomes bold to request the continuation of the divine spiritual union in which he will go on multiplying his favors in her. She declares all this in this stanza:

Do not despise me;
for if, before, you found me dark,
now truly you can look at me
since you have looked
and left in me grace and beauty" (C 33.2).

REFLECTION

When the woman was caught in adultery, she did not feel that she was beautiful. She knew that death awaited her. To make matters worse, she was brought before Jesus and to have her shame exposed to him as well. Surely, the teacher would not sacrifice his reputation to save her. Yet, Jesus found another way. He challenged her accusers to throw the first stone if they had not sin. He turned the tables on them and they walked away. Jesus did this because everyone created in his image and likeness is worthy of love. The challenge for all of us is to remember that this worthiness comes not from ourselves but from God in his inscrutable designs for us to become partakers of his divine nature.

Here is an echo of what St. Teresa says of true humility: All that we find that is good in us comes from God; all that we find evil in us comes from ourselves. The more we remember this, the more God transforms that which is ugly in us into that which is beautiful in himself. God does not seek the destruction of anyone, least of all the woman caught in adultery, but rather their transformation into himself and his beauty.

PRAYER

God, our Father, you revealed through your Son your merciful plan to forgive us and free us from the wound of original sin and make us beautiful in your sight. Grant, we ask, that even now, as we come near the end of the Season of Lent, we may not lose heart in your mercy and show our gratitude to you by following your Son on his way to the Cross, accepting in our lives the crosses you willed for us. We ask this through Jesus Christ, your Son. Amen.

GOSPEL

Jesus went to the Mount of Olives. But early in the morning he arrived again in the temple area, and all the people started coming to him, and he sat down and taught them. Then the scribes and the Pharisees brought a woman who had been caught in adultery and made her stand in the middle. They said to him, "Teacher, this woman was caught in the very act of committing adultery. Now in the law, Moses commanded us to stone such women. So what do you say?" They said this to test him, so that they could have some charge to bring against him. Jesus bent down and began to write on the ground with his finger. But when they continued asking him, he straightened up and said to them, "Let the one among you who is without sin be the first to throw a stone at her." Again he bent down and wrote on the ground. And in response, they went away one by one, beginning with the elders. So he was left alone with the woman before him. Then Jesus straightened up and said to her, "Woman, where are they? Has no one condemned you?" She replied, "No one, sir." Then Jesus said, "Neither do I condemn you. Go, and from now on do not sin any more."

JOHN 8: 1-11

ST. JOHN OF THE CROSS

The woman caught in adultery might have lamented in these words after being seized and brought to Jesus.

"Jeremiah gives vent to all these lamentations about his afflictions and trials and depicts very vividly the sufferings of a soul in this purgation and spiritual night [see also Lam 3:1–20].

"One ought to have deep compassion for the soul God puts in this tempestuous and frightful night. It may be true that the soul is fortunate because of what is being accomplished within it, for great blessings will proceed from this night; and Job affirms that out of darkness God will raise up in the soul profound blessings and change the shadow of death into light [Jb. 12:22]; and God will do this in such a way that, as David says, the light will become what the darkness was [Ps. 139:12]. Nevertheless, the soul is deserving of great pity because of the immense tribulation and the suffering of extreme uncertainty about a remedy. It believes, as Jeremiah says [Lam. 3:18], that its evil will never end. And it feels as David that God has placed it in darkness like the dead of old, and that its spirit as a result is in anguish within it and its heart troubled [Ps. 143:3-4].

"Added to this, because of the solitude and desolation this night causes, is the fact that individuals in this state find neither consolation nor support in any doctrine or spiritual master. Although their spiritual director may point out many reasons for comfort on account of the blessings contained in these afflictions, they cannot believe this. Because they are engulfed and immersed in that feeling of evil by which they so clearly see their own miseries, they believe their directors say these things because they do not understand them and do not see what they themselves see and feel. Instead of consolation they experience greater sorrow, thinking that the director's doctrine is no remedy for their evil. Indeed, it is not a remedy, for until the Lord finishes purging them in the way he desires, no remedy is a help to them in their sorrow. Their helplessness is even greater because of the little they can do in this situation. They resemble one who is imprisoned in a dark dungeon, bound hands and feet, and able neither to move nor see nor feel any favor from heaven or earth. They remain in this condition until their spirit is humbled, softened, and purified, until it becomes so delicate, simple, and refined that it can be one with the Spirit of God, according to the degree of union of love that God, in his mercy, desires to grant. In conformity with this degree, the purgation is of greater or lesser force and endures for a longer or shorter time" (N 2.7.3).

REFLECTION

In his second book on the Dark Night, John of the Cross talks about God's work in the deepest part of one's soul. Sometimes he calls this area the substance of the soul and other times he calls it the spirit. In any case, he means to tell us that when God works in this area of ourselves, we are not able to either block or aid God's work because it is God's work. It is somewhat difficult to describe because we do not have ready access to the substance of our being. We can become aware of it from time to time, but for the most part, it remains hidden to us. Maybe another way to describe this area of ourselves is to call it the bottom of who we are below are abilities to feel, sense, think or understand. We know that there is a core to ourselves but of itself, it is not accessible to us as say our thoughts or even our unconscious, which we can get some inkling of through our dreams. Some have wanted to call it our unconscious, but the core of our being, the substance or spirit or bottom is deeper even than that because it is where God is most present to us. John of the Cross describes this inner core of our being in his book, The Living Flame of Love:

"It should be known that God dwells secretly in all souls and is hidden in their substance, for otherwise they would not last. Yet there is a difference, a great difference, in his dwelling in them. In some souls he dwells alone, and in others he does not dwell alone. Abiding in some he is pleased; and in others, he is displeased. He lives in some as though in his own house, commanding and ruling everything; and in others as though a stranger in a strange house, where they do not permit him to give orders or do anything" (F 4.14).

The woman caught in adultery found herself in a frightful situation. She knew that she could be stoned to death at any time. She may have even felt that God had abandoned her and left her to the justice she deserved. However she interpreted it, it must have been a dark night for her.

Few of us undergo this type of suffering that John of the Cross describes in this book, but it should not be thought that our spirits are any less involved when we do undergo suffering from any direction in our lives. Suffering by its nature affects our whole being: physical, psychological, and even the core of who we are. For those who accept such suffering out of love for God and in a true desire to imitate Christ in his sufferings, it brings for them unimaginable treasures that affect their spirit's ability to be in God's presence. Blessed are they who can persevere through these periods in faith, hope, and charity. As John of the Cross also says in the Living Flame:

"Oh, how happy is this soul, which ever experiences God resting and reposing within it! Oh, how fitting it is for it to withdraw from things, flee from business matters, and live in immense tranquility, so that it may not, even with the slightest speck of dust or noise, disturb or trouble its heart where the Beloved dwells.

"He is usually there, in this embrace with his bride, as though asleep in the substance of the soul. And it is very well aware of him and ordinarily enjoys him. Were he always awake within it, communicating knowledge and love, it would already be in glory. For if, when he does waken, scarcely opening his eyes, he has such an effect on the soul, what would things be like were he ordinarily in it fully awake?" (F 4.15).

PRAYER

Lord God, you lead us along the right paths for your name's sake. Even if it seems that the way ahead of us is dark and foreboding, you have given us your Son to be our model of authentic living. Grant, we ask, that in such times as when we find ourselves like the woman caught in adultery or like that of your Son when he was held in prison, we may not lose faith in your presence and love for us. We ask this in Jesus' name. Amen.

In Year C, when the preceding Gospel is read on Sunday, the following text is used.

GOSPEL

Jesus spoke to them again, saying, "I am the light of the world. Whoever follows me will not walk in darkness, but will have the light of life." So the Pharisees said to him, "You testify on your own behalf, so your testimony cannot be verified." Jesus answered and said to them, "Even if I do testify on my own behalf, my testimony can be verified, because I know where I came from and where I am going. But you do not know where I come from or where I am going. You judge by appearances, but I do not judge anyone. And even if I should judge, my judgment is valid, because I am not alone, but it is I and the Father who sent me. Even in your law it is written that the testimony of two men can be verified. I testify on my behalf and so does the Father who sent me." So they said to him, "Where is your father?" Jesus answered, "You know neither me nor my Father. If you knew me, you would know my Father also." He spoke these words while teaching in the treasury in the temple area. But no one arrested him, because his hour had not yet come.

JOHN 8: 12-20

ST. JOHN OF THE CROSS

The soul's desire for the Beloved who will free her from her miseries is Christ, the Son of God, whose light will liberate her from her darkness.

"To further urge and persuade her Beloved to grant her petition, she declares that he must be the one to extinguish these miseries, since he alone suffices to satisfy her need. It is noteworthy that God is very ready to comfort and satisfy the soul in her needs and afflictions when she neither has nor desires consolation and satisfaction outside of him. The soul possessing nothing that might withhold her from God cannot remain long without a visit from her Beloved.
and may my eyes behold you,

"That is: May I see you face to face with the eyes of my soul,
because you are their light,

"In addition to the fact that God is the supernatural light of the soul's eyes, and without this light she is enveloped in darkness, she affectionately calls him here the light of her eyes, just as a lover would call her loved one the light of her eyes in order to show her affection.
"These two verses are like saying: Since my eyes have no other light (neither through nature nor through love) than you, "may my eyes behold you because you are their light" in every way. David noted the absence of this light when he lamented: The light of my eyes itself is not with me [Ps 38:10]. *Tobit did the same:* What joy can be mine, since I am seated in darkness and do not see the light of heaven? [Tb 5:12]. *Through these words he gave expression to his desire for the clear vision of God, because the light of heaven is the Son of God, as St. John says:* The heavenly city has no need of the sun or the moon to shine in it, because the brightness of God illumines it, and the Lamb is the lamp thereof [Rv 21:23]" (C 10.6–8).

REFLECTION

It may be asked, What is it that causes darkness in the life of a Christian? Many of us suffer darkness from the loss of a loved one, a job, a good opportunity, loss of health, and so forth; but these are sufferings suffered by everyone. What is it that causes darkness for the Christian? The cause of darkness for the Christian does not lie in the loss of wealth, health, or a relationship as much as the loss of the Savior, Jesus Christ, through a lack of faith. For the Christian, there is no loss comparable to the loss of Christ. Other losses can be remedied in time, but the loss of Christ cannot remedied except by conversion and the pleasure of God. This is because faith is a gift from God and it is not to be taken lightly. As long as we live by the light of faith all difficulties and all losses can be understood as our participation in the sufferings and losses of Jesus Christ. Without this light of faith, we are indeed in a great darkness.

For John of the Cross, when the soul lives by faith, not only are the difficulties and losses at least understandable, it also opens her to the love of God, that God is ready to reveal to her. As John of the Cross says, for the soul with faith, God becomes the light of her eyes, just as one person calls a friend or a love, the light of his or her eyes. The light of faith is more than just a means for coping with life's challenges. It opens up the way to a deeper life in God through Christ, the light of the world.

PRAYER

Lord God, through your Son you called us out of darkness into your wonderful light. Grant, we ask, that as we follow your Son as our Light, we may find in him all the joy he promises to those who believe in Him. We ask this through Christ, your Son. Amen.

GOSPEL

JESUS SAID TO THE PHARISEES:

"I am going away and you will look for me, but you will die in your sin. Where I am going you cannot come." So the Jews said, "He is not going to kill himself, is he, because he said, 'Where I am going you cannot come'?" He said to them, "You belong to what is below, I belong to what is above. You belong to this world, but I do not belong to this world. That is why I told you that you will die in your sins. For if you do not believe that I AM, you will die in your sins." So they said to him, "Who are you?" Jesus said to them, "What I told you from the beginning. I have much to say about you in condemnation. But the one who sent me is true, and what I heard from him I tell the world." They did not realize that he was speaking to them of the Father. So Jesus said to them, "When you lift up the Son of Man, then you will realize that I AM, and that I do nothing on my own, but I say only what the Father taught me. The one who sent me is with me. He has not left me alone, because I always do what is pleasing to him." Because he spoke this way, many came to believe in him.

JOHN 8: 21-30

ST. JOHN OF THE CROSS

In his ninth Romance, John of the Cross describes the dialogue between the Father and the Son concerning the creation of the human race.

"My Son, I wish to give you
a bride who will love you.
Because of you she will deserve
to share our company,
and eat at our table,
the same bread I eat,
that she may know the good
I have in such a Son;
and rejoice with me
in your grace and fullness."
"I am very grateful,"
the Son answered;
"I will show my brightness
to the bride you give me,
so that by it she may see
how great my Father is,
and how I have received
my being from your being.
I will hold her in my arms
and she will burn with your love,
and with eternal delight
she will exalt your goodness."
(P 9.3).

REFLECTION

It is rare that we get any inkling of what the relationship between God the Father and God the Son is like; but we can see from the quoted verse that Jesus sees himself only doing what the Father tells him, and that he says nothing unless the Father teaches him. You might say that between God the Father and the Son, there is a kind of synergy in spirit where the Son and the Father see eye to eye in one another.

In the selection from John of the Cross' poems called the Romances, we see this relationship acting between the Father's will to give his Son a gift of a bride in the human race, and the Son accepting his Father's gift with the promise to make her love the Father with the same love he has for the Father. It can be comforting to know that after all is said and done, after all the efforts in and out of Lent to lead good Christian lives, in the eyes of God, we are still his gift to his Son and we are still a gift his Son is trying to perfect for the Father.

PRAYER

God, our Father, you sent your only Son to us so that you could see and love in us what you see and love in your Son. Grant, we ask, that as we follow now your Son in his period of being persecuted by his enemies, we may also imitate him in accepting our sufferings out of love for him. We ask this in Christ, your Son's Name. Amen.

GOSPEL

Jesus said to those Jews who believed in him, "If you remain in my word, you will truly be my disciples, and you will know the truth, and the truth will set you free." They answered him, "We are descendants of Abraham and have never been enslaved to anyone. How can you say, 'You will become free'?" Jesus answered them, "Amen, amen, I say to you, everyone who commits sin is a slave of sin. A slave does not remain in a household forever, but a son always remains. So if the Son frees you, then you will truly be free. I know that you are descendants of Abraham. But you are trying to kill me, because my word has no room among you. I tell you what I have seen in the Father's presence; then do what you have heard from the Father."

They answered and said to him, "Our father is Abraham." Jesus said to them, "If you were Abraham's children, you would be doing the works of Abraham. But now you are trying to kill me, a man who has told you the truth that I heard from God; Abraham did not do this. You are doing the works of your father!" So they said to him, "We were not born of fornication. We have one Father, God." Jesus said to them, "If God were your Father, you would love me, for I came from God and am here; I did not come on my own, but he sent me."

JOHN 8: 31-42

ST. JOHN OF THE CROSS

For John of the Cross, Christ frees the soul who commits herself to him. Christ is the Bridegroom and Good Shepherd of the soul.

"Great was the desire of the Bridegroom to free and ransom his bride completely from the hands of sensuality and the devil. Like the good shepherd rejoicing and holding on his shoulders the lost sheep for which he had searched along many winding paths [Lk 15:4–5], *and like the woman who, having lit the candle and hunted through her whole house for the lost drachma, holding it up in her hands with gladness and calling her friends and neighbors to come and celebrate, saying, rejoice with me, and so on* [Lk 15:8–9], *now, too, that the soul is liberated, this loving Shepherd and Bridegroom rejoices. And it is wonderful to see his pleasure in carrying the rescued, perfected soul on his shoulders, held there by his hands in this desired union.*

"Not only does he himself rejoice, but he also makes the angels and saintly souls share in his gladness, saying in the words of the Song of Songs: Go forth, daughters of Zion, and behold king Solomon in the crown with which his mother crowned him on the day of his espousal and on the day of the joy in his heart [Sg. 3:11]. *By these words he calls the soul his crown, his bride, and the joy of his heart, and he takes her now in his arms and goes forth with her as the bridegroom from his bridal chamber* [Ps. 19:5]. *He refers to all this in the following stanza:*

> *The bride has entered*
> *the sweet garden of her desire,*
> *and she rests in delight,*
> *laying her neck*
> *on the gentle arms of her Beloved"* (C 22.1).

REFLECTION

We all have a great desire for freedom. Freedom is what makes us fully human beings. When we are not free, we feel constrained, locked in or blocked in, unable to make decisions that will further our happiness or even that of others. It is this lack of freedom with regard to God, and the things of God, that John of the Cross is most concerned about. As long as we are tied down to enjoying the good things life has to offer us, we are not free to enjoy God or the joys that God wishes to give us. One of the joys that God wishes to give us is the joy that comes from being united with him. It is the joy that he has in freeing a soul from self-love, in attaching herself to anything apart from God; and it is a joy that he shares with her and all the angels and saints as well. Blessed are those who have found this freedom won at so great a price through the death of His Son on the Cross.

PRAYER

Lord God, your Son taught that those who believe in him will be free from sin. Grant, we ask, that as we follow him through his period of persecution, we may continue to work to free ourselves by the help of his grace, from those attachments that lead us to sin. We ask this through Christ, our Lord. Amen.

GOSPEL

JESUS SAID TO THE JEWS:

"Amen, amen, I say to you, whoever keeps my word will never see death." So the Jews said to him, "Now we are sure that you are possessed. Abraham died, as did the prophets, yet you say, 'Whoever keeps my word will never taste death.' Are you greater than our father Abraham, who died? Or the prophets, who died? Who do you make yourself out to be?" Jesus answered, "If I glorify myself, my glory is worth nothing; but it is my Father who glorifies me, of whom you say, 'He is our God.' You do not know him, but I know him. And if I should say that I do not know him, I would be like you a liar. But I do know him and I keep his word. Abraham your father rejoiced to see my day; he saw it and was glad." So the Jews said to him, "You are not yet fifty years old and you have seen Abraham?" Jesus said to them, "Amen, amen, I say to you, before Abraham came to be, I AM." So they picked up stones to throw at him; but Jesus hid and went out of the temple area.

JOHN 8: 51-59

ST. JOHN OF THE CROSS

Christ, the Word of God, produces a foretaste of eternal life in the soul that believes in him.

"Finally, then, O Word, indescribably delicate touch, produced in the soul only by your most simple being that, since it is infinite, is infinitely delicate and hence touches so subtly, lovingly, eminently, and delicately,

that tastes of eternal life

"Although that which the soul tastes in this touch of God is not perfect, it does in fact have a certain savor of eternal life, as was mentioned. And this is not incredible if we believe, as we should, that this is a touch of substances, that is, of the substance of God in the substance of the soul. Many saints have attained to this substantial touch during their lives on earth.

"The delicateness of delight felt in this contact is inexpressible. I would desire not to speak of it so as to avoid giving the impression that it is no more than what I describe. There is no way to catch in words the sublime things of God that take place in these souls. The appropriate language for the persons receiving these favors is that they understand them, experience them within themselves, enjoy them, and be silent. One is conscious in this state that these things are in a certain way like the white pebble that St. John said would be given to the one who conquers: and on that pebble a new name written, which no one knows but the one who receives it [Rv 2:17]. Thus one can only say, and truthfully, "that tastes of eternal life."

"Although one does not have perfect fruition in this life as in glory, this touch, nevertheless, since it is a touch, tastes of eternal life. As a result the soul tastes here all the things of God, since God communicates to it fortitude, wisdom, love, beauty, grace, goodness, and so on. Because God is all these things, a person enjoys them in only one touch of God, and the soul rejoices within its faculties and within its substance" (F 2.20b–21).

REFLECTION

Many Christians experience life as though it were on two levels. There is the first level of our everyday life, and there is the second level of our eternal life with neither the two ever meeting. Christian revelation on the other hand collapses the two levels into one. From this point of view, the every day life that we live and the eternal life that we will one day live are going on at the same time. The only difference between the two is that the first is known from experience while the second is known through faith. As the author to the Hebrews said speaking of eternal life as rest or as a Sabbath said,

"Therefore, a sabbath rest still remains for the people of God. And whoever enters into God's rest, rests from his own works as God did from his. Therefore, let us strive to enter into that rest, so that no one may fall after the same example of disobedience" (Hebrews 4:9–11).

John in his Gospel called this eternal life, knowledge of God the Father as the true God and the one whom sent Jesus Christ (Jn 17:3) to show that for the Christian the difference between the two levels of life are only different in kind, not in the ability to know from experience the theological reality they signify.

That is why John of the Cross is open to the idea that Christians can experience eternal life from God even in this life. It may not be experienced by everybody, but it is open to all that God has chosen to experience it. It will not be like the eternal life that will be experienced in heaven, but it will contain something of the peace, love, and joy of eternal life.

PRAYER

Lord, Jesus, you promised that those who believe in you and keep your word will never see death. Grant, we ask, that, empowered with this promise, we may more easily follow you and endure suffering and persecution for your sake. We ask this dear Lord in your name. Amen.

GOSPEL

The Jews picked up rocks to stone Jesus. Jesus answered them, "I have shown you many good works from my Father. For which of these are you trying to stone me?" The Jews answered him, "We are not stoning you for a good work but for blasphemy. You, a man, are making yourself God." Jesus answered them, "Is it not written in your law, 'I said, "You are gods"'? If it calls them gods to whom the word of God came, and Scripture cannot be set aside, can you say that the one whom the Father has consecrated and sent into the world blasphemes because I said, 'I am the Son of God'? If I do not perform my Father's works, do not believe me; but if I perform them, even if you do not believe me, believe the works, so that you may realize and understand that the Father is in me and I am in the Father." Then they tried again to arrest him; but he escaped from their power.

He went back across the Jordan to the place where John first baptized, and there he remained. Many came to him and said, "John performed no sign, but everything John said about this man was true." And many there began to believe in him.

JOHN 10: 31-42

ST. JOHN OF THE CROSS

John of the Cross develops an explanation for how human beings are called to partake in the divine nature of God.

"No knowledge or power can describe how this happens (the soul becoming transformed into God), unless by explaining how the Son of God attained and merited such a high state for us, the power to be children of God, as St. John says [Jn 1:12]. Thus the Son asked of the Father in St. John's

Gospel: Father, I desire that where I am those you have given me may also be with me, that they may see the glory you have given me [Jn 17:24], *that is, that they may perform in us by participation the same work that I do by nature; that is, breathe the Holy Spirit. And he adds:* I do not ask, Father, only for those present, but for those also who will believe in me through their doctrine; that all of them may be one as you, Father, in me and I in you, that thus they be one in us. The glory which you have given me I have given them that they may be one as we are one, I in them and you in me; that they may be perfect in one; that the world may know that you have sent me and loved them as you have loved me [Jn 17:20–23]. *The Father loves them by communicating to them the same love he communicates to the Son, though not naturally as to the Son but, as we said, through unity and transformation of love. It should not be thought that the Son desires here to ask the Father that the saints be one with him essentially and naturally as the Son is with the Father, but that they may be so through the union of love, just as the Father and the Son are one in unity of love.*

"Accordingly, souls possess the same goods by participation that the Son possesses by nature. As a result they are truly gods by participation, equals and companions of God. Wherefore St. Peter said: May grace and peace be accomplished and perfect in you in the knowledge of God and of our Lord Jesus Christ, as all things of his divine power that pertain to life and piety are given us through the knowledge of him who called us with his own glory and power, by whom he has given us very great and precious promises, that by these we may be made partakers of the divine nature [2 Pt 1:2–4]. *These are words from St. Peter in which he clearly indicates that the soul will participate in God himself by performing in him, in company with him, the work of the Most Blessed Trinity because of the substantial union between the soul and God. Although this participation will be perfectly accomplished in the next life, still in this life when the soul has reached the state of perfection, as has the soul we are here discussing, she obtains a foretaste and noticeable trace of it in the way we are describing, although as we said it is indescribable"* (C 39.5–6).

REFLECTION

Another polarity Christians often experience in their lives is the moral and the mystical. The moral is what most people are expected to live while the mystical is what few, if anybody, can hope to live. While it is generally true in our experience, it is not true from the point of view of revelation. As John of the Cross shows, the mystical life is a gift that God gives to all who believe in Jesus, as sent by the Father and who in turn makes all believers one in himself, so that they could be one with the Father as he is one with the Father (Jn. 17:20–23). John of the Cross also goes on to quote 2 Pt 1:2–4 where Peter says that we are called to become partakers of God's nature. Thus, what the Son shares essentially with the Father, Christians share by way of participation in the divine life that Christ came to bring. This life that Jesus came to bring was fraught with suffering due to persecution for maintaining that he had come from the Father and that he was his Son. As we prepare now for Holy Week, let us make our own the sufferings Jesus endured, so that we could become coheirs (Eph 3:6) with him by accepting our own sufferings.

PRAYER

Lord God, you sent your Son so that all who believe in him would have the power to become your children. Grant, we ask, that as we struggle to share in his sufferings, we may also know ourselves to be partakers of his divine life in you. We ask this through Christ our Lord. Amen.

GOSPEL

Many of the Jews who had come to Mary and seen what Jesus had done began to believe in him. But some of them went to the Pharisees and told them what Jesus had done. So the chief priests and the Pharisees convened the Sanhedrin and said, "What are we going to do? This man is performing many signs. If we leave him alone, all will believe in him, and the Romans will come and take away both our land and our nation." But one of them, Caiaphas, who was high priest that year, said to them "You know nothing, nor do you consider that it is better for you that one man should die instead of the people, so that the whole nation may not perish." He did not say this on his own, but since he was high priest for that year, he prophesied that Jesus was going to die for the nation, and not only for the nation, but also to gather into one the dispersed children of God. So from that day on they planned to kill him.

So Jesus no longer walked about in public among the Jews, but he left for the region near the desert, to a town called Ephraim, and there he remained with his disciples.

Now the Passover of the Jews was near, and many went up from the country to Jerusalem before Passover to purify themselves. They looked for Jesus and said to one another as they were in the temple area, "What do you think? That he will not come to the feast?"

JOHN 11: 45-56

ST. JOHN OF THE CROSS

John of the Cross uses the occasion of Caiaphas' prophecy to teach that it is very difficult to interpret locutions in prayer.

"The Holy Spirit causes many things to be said in which he has a meaning different from that understood by humans. This is seen by what he

brought Caiaphas to say of Christ: It is better that one man die than that the whole nation perish [Jn 11:50]. *Caiaphas did not say these words on his own, and he expressed and understood them in one way while the Holy Spirit did so in another.*

"Evidently, then, even though the words and revelations are from God we cannot find assurance in them, since in our understanding of them we can easily be deluded, and very much so. They embody an abyss and depth of spirit, and to want to limit them to our interpretation and to what our senses can apprehend is like wanting to grasp a handful of air that will escape the hand entirely, leaving only a particle of dust" (A 2.19.9c–10).

REFLECTION

In today's Gospel, Caiaphas declares that it is better for one man (Jesus) to die than for the whole nation to perish. Caiaphas did not know it at the time, but he was not speaking as himself but as high priest and thus made a prophetic statement. As John of the Cross observed, Caiaphas meant to be understood one way but the Holy Spirit meant it to be understood in another way. From this John of the Cross teaches that locutions and visions about the future can be very deceptive as they come from God and thus always mean more than we can grasp. The important thing in all this is that Jesus, in being the definitive Word of the Father, has freed us from speculations about future events. We only need to follow him in the ordinary experiences of our lives.

PRAYER

Lord, God, you willed that your Son should suffer and die for our salvation. Grant, we ask, that we may always trust in him whom you have sent, so that we may share in the eternal life he promised us. We ask this, through Christ your Son and our Lord. Amen.

HOLY
WEEK

GOSPEL

AT THE PROCESSION WITH PALMS

When Jesus and the disciples drew near Jerusalem and came to Bethphage on the Mount of Olives, Jesus sent two disciples, saying to them, "Go into the village opposite you, and immediately you will find an ass tethered, and a colt with her. Untie them and bring them here to me. And if anyone should say anything to you, reply, 'The master has need of them.' Then he will send them at once." This happened so that what had been spoken through the prophet might be fulfilled: / *Say to daughter Zion,* / *"Behold, your king comes to you,* / *meek and riding on an ass,* / *and on a colt, the foal of a beast of burden."* / The disciples went and did as Jesus had ordered them. They brought the ass and the colt and laid their cloaks over them, and he sat upon them. The very large crowd spread their cloaks on the road, while others cut branches from the trees and strewed them on the road. The crowds preceding him and those following kept crying out and saying: / "Hosanna to the Son of David; / blessed is the he who comes in the name of the Lord; / hosanna in the highest." / And when he entered Jerusalem the whole city was shaken and asked, "Who is this?" And the crowds replied, "This is Jesus the prophet, from Nazareth in Galilee."

MATTHEW 21: 1-11

GOSPEL

MASS

One of the Twelve, who was called Judas Iscariot, went to the chief priests and said, "What are you willing to give me if I hand him over to you?" They paid him thirty pieces of silver, and from that time on he looked for an opportunity to hand him over.

On the first day of the Feast of Unleavened Bread, the disciples approached Jesus and said, "Where do you want us to prepare for you to eat the Passover?" He said, "Go into the city to a certain man and tell him, 'The teacher says, "My appointed time draws near; in your house I shall celebrate the Passover with my disciples."'" The disciples then did as Jesus had ordered, and prepared the Passover.

When it was evening, he reclined at table with the Twelve. And while they were eating, he said, "Amen, I say to you, one of you will betray me." Deeply distressed at this, they began to say to him one after another, "Surely it is not I, Lord?" He said in reply, "He who has dipped his hand into the dish with me is the one who will betray me. The Son of Man indeed goes, as it is written of him, but woe to that man by whom the Son of Man is betrayed. It would be better for that man if he had never been born." Then Judas, his betrayer, said in reply, "Surely it is not I, Rabbi?" He answered, "You have said so."

While they were eating, Jesus took bread, said the blessing, broke it, and giving it to his disciples said, "Take and eat; this is my body." Then he took a cup, gave thanks, and gave it to them, saying, "Drink from it, all of you, for this is my blood of the covenant, which will be shed on behalf of many for the forgiveness of sins. I tell you, from now on I shall not drink this fruit of the vine until the day when I drink it with you new in the kingdom of my Father." Then, after singing a hymn, they went out to the Mount of Olives.

Then Jesus said to them, "This night all of you will have your faith in me shaken, for it is written: / *I will strike the shepherd, / and the sheep of the flock will be dispersed;* / but after I have been raised up, I shall go before you to Galilee." Peter said to him in reply, "Though all may have their faith in you shaken, mine will never be." Jesus said to him, "Amen, I say to you, this very night before the cock crows, you will deny me three times." Peter said to him, "Even though I should have to die with you, I will not deny you." And all the disciples spoke likewise.

Then Jesus came with them to a place called Gethsemane, and he said to his disciples, "Sit here while I go over there and pray." He took along Peter and the two sons of Zebedee, and began to feel sorrow and distress. Then he said to them, "My soul is sorrowful even to death. Remain here and keep watch with me." He advanced a little and fell prostrate in prayer, saying, "My Father, if it is possible, let this cup pass from me; yet, not as I will, but as you will." When he returned to his disciples he found them asleep. He said to Peter, "So you could not keep watch with me for one hour? Watch and pray that you may not undergo the test. The spirit is willing, but the flesh is weak." Withdrawing a second time, he prayed again, "My Father, if it is not possible that this cup pass without my drinking it, your will be done!" Then he returned once more and found them asleep, for they could not keep their eyes open. He left them and withdrew again and prayed a third time, saying the same thing again. Then he returned to his disciples and said to them, "Are you still sleeping and taking your rest? Behold, the hour is at hand when the Son of Man is to be handed over to sinners. Get up, let us go. Look, my betrayer is at hand."

While he was still speaking, Judas, one of the Twelve, arrived, accompanied by a large crowd, with swords and clubs, who had come from the chief priests and the elders of the people. His betrayer had arranged a sign with them, saying, "The man I shall kiss is the one; arrest him." Immediately he went over to Jesus and said, "Hail, Rabbi!" and he kissed him. Jesus answered him, "Friend, do what you have come for." Then stepping forward they laid hands on Jesus and arrested him. And behold, one of those who accompanied Jesus put his hand to his sword, drew it, and struck the high priest's servant, cutting off his ear. Then Jesus said to him, "Put your sword back into its sheath, for all who take the sword will perish by the sword. Do you think that I cannot call upon my Father and he will not provide me at this moment with more than twelve legions of angels? But then how would the Scriptures be fulfilled which say that it must come to pass in this way?" At that hour Jesus said to the crowds, "Have you come out as against a robber, with swords and clubs to seize me? Day after day I sat teaching in the temple area, yet you did not arrest me. But all this has come to pass that the writings of the prophets may be fulfilled." Then all the disciples left him and fled.

Those who had arrested Jesus led him away to Caiaphas the high priest, where the scribes and the elders were assembled. Peter was following him at a distance as far as the high priest's courtyard, and going inside he sat down with the servants to see the outcome. The chief priests and the entire Sanhedrin kept trying to obtain false testimony against Jesus in order to put him to death, but they found none, though many false witnesses came forward. Finally two came forward who stated, "This man said, 'I can destroy the temple of God and within three days rebuild it.'" The high priest rose and addressed him, "Have you no answer? What are these men testifying against you?" But Jesus was silent. Then the high priest said to him, "I order you to tell us under oath before the living God whether you are the Christ, the Son of God." Jesus said to him in reply, "You have said so. But I tell you: / From now on you will see 'the Son of Man / seated at the right hand of the Power' / and 'coming on the clouds of heaven.'" / Then the high priest tore his robes and said, "He has blasphemed! What further need have we of witnesses? You have now heard the blasphemy; what is your opinion?" They said in reply, "He deserves to die!" Then they spat in his face and struck him, while some slapped him, saying, "Prophesy for us, Christ: who is it that struck you?"

Now Peter was sitting outside in the courtyard. One of the maids came over to him and said, "You too were with Jesus the Galilean." But he denied it in front of everyone, saying, "I do not know what you are talking about!" As he went out to the gate, another girl saw him and said to those who were there, "This man was with Jesus the Nazorean." Again he denied it with an oath, "I do not know the man!" A little later the bystanders came over and said to Peter, "Surely you too are one of them; even your speech gives you away." At that he began to curse and to swear, "I do not know the man." And immediately a cock crowed. Then Peter remembered the word that Jesus had spoken: "Before the cock crows you will deny me three times." He went out and began to weep bitterly.

When it was morning, all the chief priests and the elders of the people took counsel against Jesus to put him to death. They bound him, led him away, and handed him over to Pilate, the governor.

Then Judas, his betrayer, seeing that Jesus had been condemned, deeply regretted what he had done. He returned the thirty pieces of silver to the chief priests and elders, saying, "I have sinned in betraying innocent blood." They said, "What is that to us? Look to it yourself." Flinging the money into the temple, he departed and went off and hanged himself. The chief priests gathered up the money, but said, "It is not lawful to deposit this in the temple treasury, for it is the price of blood." After consultation, they used it to buy the potter's field as a burial place for foreigners. That is why that field even today is called the Field of Blood. Then was fulfilled what had been said through Jeremiah the prophet, / *And they took the thirty pieces of silver, / the value of a man with a price on his head, / a price set by some of the Israelites, / and they paid it out for the potter's field / just as the Lord had commanded me.*

Now Jesus stood before the governor, who questioned him, "Are you the king of the Jews?" Jesus said, "You say so." And when he was accused by the chief priests and elders, he made no answer. Then Pilate said to him, "Do you not hear how many things they are testifying against you?" But he did not answer him one word, so that the governor was greatly amazed.

Now on the occasion of the feast the governor was accustomed to release to the crowd one prisoner whom they wished. And at that time they had a notorious prisoner called Barabbas. So when they had assembled, Pilate said to them, "Which one do you want me to release to you, Barabbas, or Jesus called Christ?" For he knew that it was out of envy that they had handed him over. While he was still seated on the bench, his wife sent him a message, "Have nothing to do with that righteous man. I suffered much in a dream today because of him." The chief priests and the elders persuaded the crowds to ask for Barabbas but to destroy Jesus. The governor said to them in reply, "Which of the two do you want me to release to you?" They answered, "Barabbas!" Pilate said to them, "Then what shall I do with Jesus called Christ?" They all said, "Let him be crucified!" But he said, "Why? What evil has he done?" They only shouted the louder, "Let him be crucified!" When Pilate saw that he was not succeeding at all, but that a riot was breaking out instead, he took water and washed his hands in the sight of the crowd, saying, "I am innocent of this man's blood. Look to it yourselves." And the whole people said in reply, "His blood be upon us and upon our children." Then he released Barabbas to them, but after he had Jesus scourged, he handed him over to be crucified.

Then the soldiers of the governor took Jesus inside the praetorium and gathered the whole cohort around him. They stripped off his clothes and threw a scarlet military cloak about him. Weaving a crown out of thorns, they placed it on his head, and a reed in his right hand. And kneeling before him, they mocked him, saying, "Hail, King of the Jews!" They spat upon him and took the reed and kept striking him on the head. And when they had mocked him, they stripped him of the cloak, dressed him in his own clothes, and led him off to crucify him.

As they were going out, they met a Cyrenian named Simon; this man they pressed into service to carry his cross.

And when they came to a place called Golgotha — which means Place of the Skull —, they gave Jesus wine to drink mixed with gall. But when he had tasted it, he refused to drink. After they had crucified him, they divided his garments by casting lots; then they sat down and kept watch over him there. And they placed over his head the written charge against him: This is Jesus, the King of the Jews. Two revolutionaries were crucified with him, one on his right and the other on his left. Those passing by reviled him, shaking their heads and saying, "You who would destroy the temple and rebuild it in three days, save yourself, if you are the Son of God, and come down from the cross!" Likewise the chief priests with the scribes and elders mocked him and said, "He saved others; he cannot save himself. So he is the king of Israel! Let him come down from the cross now, and we will believe in him. He trusted in God; let him deliver him now if he wants him. For he said, 'I am the Son of God.'" The revolutionaries who were crucified with him also kept abusing him in the same way.

From noon onward, darkness came over the whole land until three in the afternoon. And about three o'clock Jesus cried out in a loud voice, *"Eli, Eli, lema sabachthani?"* which means, "My God, my God, why have you forsaken me?" Some of the bystanders who heard it said, "This one is calling for Elijah." Immediately one of them ran to get a sponge; he soaked it in wine, and putting it on a reed, gave it to him to drink. But the rest said, "Wait, let us see if Elijah comes to save him." But Jesus cried out again in a loud voice, and gave up his spirit.

Here all kneel and pause for a short time.

· And behold, the veil of the sanctuary was torn in two from top to bottom. The earth quaked, rocks were split, tombs were opened, and the bodies of many saints who had fallen asleep were raised. And coming forth from their tombs after his resurrection, they entered the holy city and appeared to many. The centurion and the men with him who were keeping watch over Jesus feared greatly when they saw the earthquake and all that was happening, and they said, "Truly, this was the Son of God!" There were many women there, looking on from a distance, who had followed Jesus from Galilee, ministering to him. Among them were Mary Magdalene and Mary the mother of James and Joseph, and the mother of the sons of Zebedee.

When it was evening, there came a rich man from Arimathea named Joseph, who was himself a disciple of Jesus. He went to Pilate and asked for the body of Jesus; then Pilate ordered it to be handed over. Taking the body, Joseph wrapped it in clean linen and laid it in his new tomb that he had hewn in the rock. Then he rolled a huge stone across the entrance to the tomb and departed. But Mary Magdalene and the other Mary remained sitting there, facing the tomb.

The next day, the one following the day of preparation, the chief priests and the Pharisees gathered before Pilate and said, "Sir, we remember that this impostor while still alive said, 'After three days I will be raised up.' Give orders, then, that the grave be secured until the third day, lest his disciples come and steal him and say to the people, 'He has been raised from the dead.' This last imposture would be worse than the first." Pilate said to them, "The guard is yours; go, secure it as best you can." So they went and secured the tomb by fixing a seal to the stone and setting the guard.

MATTHEW 26: 14-75 & 27: 1-66

Shorter form: MATTHEW 27:11-54

ST. JOHN OF THE CROSS

For John of the Cross, the Incarnation of the Son of God and his death on the Cross are a part of one another.

"In this high state of spiritual marriage the Bridegroom reveals his wonderful secrets to the soul as to his faithful consort, with remarkable ease and frequency, for true and perfect love knows not how to keep anything hidden from the beloved. He mainly communicates to her sweet mysteries of his Incarnation and the ways of the redemption of humankind, one of the loftiest of his works and thus more delightful to the soul. Even though he communicates many other mysteries to her, the Bridegroom in the following stanza mentions only the Incarnation as the most important. In speaking to the soul he says:

Beneath the apple tree:
there I took you for my own,
there I offered you my hand, and restored you,
where your mother was corrupted.

Commentary

"The Bridegroom explains to the soul in this stanza his admirable plan in redeeming and espousing her to himself through the very means by which human nature was corrupted and ruined, telling her that as human nature was ruined through Adam and corrupted by means of the forbidden tree in the Garden of Paradise, so on the tree of the cross it was redeemed and restored when he gave it there, through his passion and death, the hand of his favor and mercy, and broke down the barriers between God and humans that were built up through original sin" (C 23.1–2).

REFLECTION

Like the Gospels, the Season of Lent converges on the Passion Narrative of our Lord Jesus Christ. Each Gospel has its own theological outlook on the event. Today we hear the account in Matthew. For Matthew, the theological reason for Jesus' suffering and death in obedience to the Father's will was for the forgiveness of sins. For both Matthew and John, Jesus' death restores the relationship between God and human beings that has been wounded by sin.

PRAYER

Lord Jesus, your self-emptying at your birth was the beginning of your work of redemption, which you brought to completion by your self-emptying death on the cross. Grant, we ask, that, as we follow you now during Passion Week, we may see in our crosses a share in your own to make us partakers of your divine nature. We ask this dear Lord in your name. Amen.

GOSPEL

PROCESSION WITH PALMS

When Jesus and his disciples drew near to Jerusalem, to Bethpage and Bethany at the Mount of Olives, he sent two of his disciples and said to them, "Go into the village opposite you, and immediately on entering it, you will find a colt tethered on which no one has ever sat. Untie it and bring it here. If anyone should say to you, 'Why are you doing this?' reply, 'The Master has need of it and will send it back here at once.'" So they went off and found a colt tethered at a gate outside on the street, and they untied it. Some of the bystanders said to them, "What are you doing, untying the colt?" They answered them just as Jesus had told them to, and they permitted them to do it. So they brought the colt to Jesus and put their cloaks over it. And he sat on it. Many people spread their cloaks on the road, and others spread leafy branches that they had cut from the fields. Those preceding him as well as those following kept crying out: / "Hosanna! / Blessed is he who comes in the name of the Lord! / Blessed is the kingdom of our father David that is to come! / Hosanna in the highest!"

MARK 11: 1-10

Alternative: JOHN 12:12-16

GOSPEL

MASS

The Passover and the Feast of Unleavened Bread were to take place in two days' time. So the chief priests and the scribes were seeking a way to arrest him by treachery and put him to death. They said, "Not during the festival, for fear that there may be a riot among the people."

When he was in Bethany reclining at table in the house of Simon the leper, a woman came with an alabaster jar of perfumed oil, costly genuine spikenard. She broke the alabaster jar and poured it on his head. There were some who were indignant. "Why has there been this waste of perfumed oil? It could have been sold for more than three hundred days' wages and the money given to the poor." They were infuriated with her. Jesus said, "Let her alone. Why do you make trouble for her? She has done a good thing for me. The poor you will always have with you, and whenever you wish you can do good to them, but you will not always have me. She has done what she could. She has anticipated anointing my body for burial. Amen, I say to you, wherever the gospel is proclaimed to the whole world, what she has done will be told in memory of her."

Then Judas Iscariot, one of the Twelve, went off to the chief priests to hand him over to them. When they heard him they were pleased and promised to pay him money. Then he looked for an opportunity to hand him over.

On the first day of the Feast of Unleavened Bread, when they sacrificed the Passover lamb, his disciples said to him, "Where do you want us to go and prepare for you to eat the Passover?" He sent two of his disciples and said to them, "Go into a city and a man will meet you, carrying a jar of water. Follow him. Wherever he enters, say to the master of the house, 'The Teacher says, "Where is my guest room where I may eat the Passover with my disciples?"' Then he will show you a large upper room furnished and ready. Make the preparations for us there." The disciples then went off, entered the city, and found it just as he had told them; and they prepared the Passover.

When it was evening, he came with the Twelve. And as they reclined at table and were eating, Jesus said, "Amen, I say to you, one of you will betray me, one who is eating with me." They began to be distressed and to say to him, one by one, "Surely it is not I?" He said to them, "One of the Twelve, the one who dips with me into the dish. For the Son of Man indeed goes, as it is written of him, but woe to that man by whom the Son of Man is betrayed. It would be better for that man if he had never been born."

While they were eating, he took bread, said the blessing, broke it, and gave it to them, and said, "Take it; this is my body." Then he took a cup, gave thanks, and gave it to them, and they all drank from it. He said to them, "This is my blood of the covenant, which will be shed for many. Amen, I say to you, I shall not drink again the fruit of the vine until the day when I drink it new in the kingdom of God." Then, after singing a hymn, they went out to the Mount of Olives.

Then Jesus said to them, "All of you will have your faith shaken, for it is written: / *I will strike the shepherd,* / *and the sheep will be dispersed.* / But after I have been raised up, I shall go before you to Galilee." Peter said to him, "Even though all should have their faith shaken, mine will not be." Then Jesus said to him, "Amen, I say to you, this very night before the cock crows twice you will deny me three times." But he vehemently replied, "Even though I should have to die with you, I will not deny you." And they all spoke similarly.

Then they came to a place named Gethsemane, and he said to his disciples, "Sit here while I pray." He took with him Peter, James and John, and began to be troubled and distressed. Then he said to them, "My soul is sorrowful even to death. Remain here and keep watch." He advanced a little and fell to the ground and prayed that if it were possible the hour might pass by him; he said, "Abba, Father, all things are possible to you. Take this cup away from me, but not what I will but what you will." When he returned he found them asleep. He said to Peter, "Simon, are you asleep? Could you not keep watch for one hour? Watch and pray that you may not undergo the test. The spirit is willing but the flesh is weak." Withdrawing again, he prayed, saying the same thing. Then he returned once more and found them asleep, for they could not keep their eyes open and did not know what to answer him. He returned a third time and said to them, "Are you still sleeping and taking your rest? It is enough. The hour has come. Behold, the Son of Man is to be handed over to sinners. Get up, let us go. See, my betrayer is at hand."

Then, while he was still speaking, Judas, one of the Twelve, arrived, accompanied by a crowd with swords and clubs who had come from the chief priests, the scribes, and the elders. His betrayer had arranged a signal with them, saying, "The man I shall kiss is the one; arrest him and lead him away securely." He came and immediately went over to him and said, "Rabbi." And he kissed him. At this they laid hands on him and arrested him. One of the bystanders drew his sword, struck the high priest's servant, and cut off his ear. Jesus said to them in reply, "Have you come out as against a robber, with swords and clubs, to seize me? Day after day I was with you teaching in the temple area, yet you did not arrest me; but that the Scriptures may be fulfilled." And they all left him and fled. Now a young man followed him wearing nothing but a linen cloth about his body. They seized him, but he left the cloth behind and ran off naked.

They led Jesus away to the high priest, and all the chief priests and the elders and the scribes came together. Peter followed him at a distance into the high priest's courtyard and was seated with the guards, warming himself at the fire. The chief priests and the entire Sanhedrin kept trying to obtain testimony against Jesus in order to put him to death, but they found none. Many gave false witness against him, but their testimony did not agree. Some took the stand and testified falsely against him, alleging, "We heard him say, 'I will destroy this temple made with hands and within three days I will build another not made with hands.'" Even so their testimony did not agree. The high priest rose before the assembly and questioned Jesus, saying, "Have you no answer? What are these men testifying against you?" But he was silent and answered nothing. Again the high priest asked him and said to him, "Are you the Christ, the son of the Blessed One?" Then Jesus answered, "I am; / and *you will see the Son of Man / seated at the right hand of the Power / and coming with the clouds of heaven."* / At that the high priest tore his garments and said, "What further need have we of witnesses? You have heard the blasphemy. What do you think?" They all condemned him as deserving to die. Some began to spit on him. They blindfolded him and struck him and said to him, "Prophesy!" And the guards greeted him with blows.

While Peter was below in the courtyard, one of the high priest's maids came along. Seeing Peter warming himself, she looked intently at him and said, "You too were with the Nazarene, Jesus." But he denied it saying, "I neither know nor understand what you are talking about." So he went out into the outer court. Then the cock crowed. The maid saw him and began again to say to the bystanders, "This man is one of them." Once again he denied it. A little later the bystanders said to Peter once more, "Surely you are one of them; for you too are a Galilean." He began to curse and to swear, "I do not know this man about whom you are talking." And immediately a cock crowed a second time. Then Peter remembered the word that Jesus had said to him, "Before the cock crows twice you will deny me three times." He broke down and wept.

As soon as morning came, the chief priests with the elders and the scribes, that is, the whole Sanhedrin held a council. They bound Jesus, led him away, and handed him over to Pilate. Pilate questioned him, "Are you the king of the Jews?" He said to him in reply, "You say so." The chief priests accused him of many things. Again Pilate questioned him, "Have you no answer? See how many things they accuse you of." Jesus gave him no further answer, so that Pilate was amazed.

Now on the occasion of the feast he used to release to them one prisoner whom they requested. A man called Barabbas was then in prison along with the rebels who had committed murder in a rebellion. The crowd came forward and began to ask him to do for them as he was accustomed. Pilate answered, "Do you want me to release to you the king of the Jews?" For he knew that it was out of envy that the chief priests had handed him over. But the chief priests stirred up the crowd to have him release Barabbas for them instead. Pilate again said to them in reply, "Then what do you want me to do with the man you call the king of the Jews?" They shouted again, "Crucify him." Pilate said to them, "Why? What evil has he done?" They only shouted the louder, "Crucify him." So Pilate, wishing to satisfy the crowd, released Barabbas to them and, after he had Jesus scourged, handed him over to be crucified.

The soldiers led him away inside the palace, that is, the praetorium, and assembled the whole cohort. They clothed him in purple and, weaving a crown of thorns, placed it on him. They began to salute him with, "Hail, King of the Jews!" and kept striking his head with a reed and spitting upon him. They knelt before him in homage. And when they had mocked him, they stripped him of the purple cloak, dressed him in his own clothes, and led him out to crucify him.

They pressed into service a passer-by, Simon, a Cyrenian, who was coming in from the country, the father of Alexander and Rufus, to carry his cross. They brought him to the place of Golgotha—which is translated Place of the Skull—. They gave him wine drugged with myrrh, but he did not take it. Then they crucified him and divided his garments by casting lots for them to see what each should take. It was nine o'clock in the morning when they crucified him. The inscription of the charge against him read, "The King of the Jews." With him they crucified two revolutionaries, one on his right and one on his left. Those passing by reviled him, shaking their heads and saying, "Aha! You who would destroy the temple and rebuild it in three days, save yourself by coming down from the cross." Likewise the chief priests, with the scribes, mocked him among themselves and said, "He saved others; he cannot save himself. Let the Christ, the King of Israel, come down now from the cross that we may see and believe." Those who were crucified with him also kept abusing him. At noon darkness came over the whole land until three in the afternoon. And at three o'clock Jesus cried out in a loud voice, *"Eloi, Eloi, lema sabachthani?"* which is translated, "My God, my God, why have you forsaken me?" Some of the bystanders who heard it said, "Look, he is calling Elijah." One of them ran, soaked a sponge with wine, put it on a reed and gave it to him to drink saying, "Wait, let us see if Elijah comes to take him down." Jesus gave a loud cry and breathed his last.

Here all kneel and pause for a short time.

The veil of the sanctuary was torn in two from top to bottom. When the centurion who stood facing him saw how he breathed his last he said, "Truly this man was the Son of God!"

There were also women looking on from a distance. Among them were Mary Magdalene, Mary the mother of the younger James and of Joses, and Salome. These women had followed him when he was in Galilee and ministered to him. There were also many other women who had come up with him to Jerusalem.

When it was already evening, since it was the day of preparation, the day before the sabbath, Joseph of Arimathea, a distinguished member of the council, who was himself awaiting the kingdom of God, came and courageously went to Pilate and asked for the body of Jesus. Pilate was amazed that he was already dead. He summoned the centurion and asked him if Jesus had already died. And when he learned of it from the centurion, he gave the body to Joseph. Having bought a linen cloth, he took him down, wrapped him in the linen cloth, and laid him in a tomb that had been hewn out of the rock. Then he rolled a stone against the entrance to the tomb. Mary Magdalene and Mary the mother of Joses watched where he was laid.

MARK 14: 1-72 & 15: 1-47

Shorter form: MARK 15:1-39

ST. JOHN OF THE CROSS

John of the Cross continues to link the Incarnation with our Lord's death on the Cross.

"Beneath the apple tree:

"That is: beneath the favor of the tree of the cross (referred to by the apple tree), where the Son of God redeemed human nature and consequently espoused it to himself, and then espoused each soul by giving it through the cross grace and pledges for this espousal. And thus he says:
>   *there I took you for my own,*
>   *there I offered you my hand,*

"That is: There I offered you my kind regard and help by raising you from your low state to be my companion and spouse.
>   *and restored you,*
>   *where your mother was corrupted.*

"For human nature, your mother, was corrupted in your first parents under the tree, and you too under the tree of the cross were restored. If your mother, therefore, brought you death under the tree, I brought you life under the tree of the cross. In such a way God manifests the decrees of his wisdom; he knows how to draw good from evil so wisely and beautifully, and to ordain to a greater good what was a cause of evil.

"The Bridegroom himself literally speaks this stanza to the bride in the Song of Songs: Sub arbore malo suscitavi te; ibi corrupta est mater tua, ibi violata est genitrix tua *(Under the apple tree I raised you up; there your mother was corrupted, there she who bore you was violated)* [Sg 8:5]"(C 23.3–5).

REFLECTION

Like the Gospels, the Season of Lent converges on the Passion Narrative of our Lord Jesus Christ. Each Gospel has its own theological outlook on the event. For Mark, the theological reason for Jesus' suffering and death in obedience to the Father's will was done to promote the Kingdom of God: *Then he took a cup, gave thanks, and gave it to them, and they all drank from it. He said to them, "This is my blood of the covenant, which will be shed for many. Amen, I say to you, I shall not drink again the fruit of the vine until the day when I drink it new in the kingdom of God* [Mk 14:23–25]."

For Mark, the Kingdom of God is the love and will of God ruling in the hearts and minds of human beings. It is the Law of God engraved in their hearts, in the words of Jeremiah. For John of the Cross, the Kingdom of God has become an interiorized marital relationship of the soul and God. Eventually the soul becomes so freed from her self-seeking and self-loving that she becomes more and more uninhibited in her love for God and in doing God's will.

PRAYER

Lord Jesus, by your death on the Cross you restored to us the loving relationship our parents lost with God through sin. Grant, we ask, that, as we follow you in your sufferings through Passion Week, we may remember what it cost you to restore what our first parents lost, and express our gratitude by living virtuous lives and carrying faithfully the crosses your Father entrusts to us. We ask this dear Lord in your name. Amen.

Gospel

Procession with Palms

Jesus proceeded on his journey up to Jerusalem. As he drew near to Bethpage and Bethany at the place called the Mount of Olives, he sent two of his disciples. He said, "Go into the village opposite you, and as you enter it you will find a colt tethered on which no one has ever sat. Untie it and bring it here. And if anyone should ask you, 'Why are you untying it?' you will answer, 'The Master has need of it.'" So those who had been sent went off and found everything just as he had told them. And as they were untying the colt, its owner said to them, "Why are you untying this colt?" They answered, "The Master has need of it." So they brought it to Jesus, threw their cloaks over the colt, and helped Jesus to mount. As he rode along, the people were spreading their cloaks on the road; and now as he was approaching the slope of the Mount of Olives, the whole multitude of his disciples began to praise God aloud with joy for all the mighty deeds they had seen. They proclaimed: / "Blessed is the king who comes in the name of the Lord. / Peace in heaven and glory in the highest." / Some of the Pharisees in the crowd said to him, "Teacher, rebuke your disciples." He said in reply, "I tell you, if they keep silent, the stones will cry out!"

LUKE 19: 28-40

GOSPEL

MASS

When the hour came, Jesus took his place at table with the apostles. He said to them, "I have eagerly desired to eat this Passover with you before I suffer, for, I tell you, I shall not eat it again until there is fulfillment in the kingdom of God." Then he took a cup, gave thanks, and said, "Take this and share it among yourselves; for I tell you that from this time on I shall not drink of the fruit of the vine until the kingdom of God comes." Then he took the bread, said the blessing, broke it, and gave it to them, saying, "This is my body, which will be given for you; do this in memory of me." And likewise the cup after they had eaten, saying, "This cup is the new covenant in my blood, which will be shed for you.

"And yet behold, the hand of the one who is to betray me is with me on the table; for the Son of Man indeed goes as it has been determined; but woe to that man by whom he is betrayed." And they began to debate among themselves who among them would do such a deed.

Then an argument broke out among them about which of them should be regarded as the greatest. He said to them, "The kings of the Gentiles lord it over them and those in authority over them are addressed as 'Benefactors'; but among you it shall not be so. Rather, let the greatest among you be as the youngest, and the leader as the servant. For who is greater: the one seated at table or the one who serves? Is it not the one seated at table? I am among you as the one who serves. It is you who have stood by me in my trials; and I confer a kingdom on you, just as my Father has conferred one on me, that you may eat and drink at my table in my kingdom; and you will sit on thrones judging the twelve tribes of Israel.

"Simon, Simon, behold Satan has demanded to sift all of you like wheat, but I have prayed that your own faith may not fail; and once you have turned back, you must strengthen your brothers." He said to him, "Lord, I am prepared to go to prison and to die with you." But he replied, "I tell you, Peter, before the cock crows this day, you will deny three times that you know me."

He said to them, "When I sent you forth without a money bag or a sack or sandals, were you in need of anything?" "No, nothing," they replied. He said to them, "But now one who has a money bag should take it, and likewise a sack, and one who does not have a sword should sell his cloak and buy one. For I tell you that this Scripture must be fulfilled in me, namely, *He was counted among the wicked;* and indeed what is written about me is coming to fulfillment." Then they said, "Lord, look, there are two swords here." But he replied, "It is enough!"

Then going out, he went, as was his custom, to the Mount of Olives, and the disciples followed him. When he arrived at the place he said to them, "Pray that you may not undergo the test." After withdrawing about a stone's throw from them and kneeling, he prayed, saying, "Father, if you are willing, take this cup away from me; still, not my will but yours be done." And to strengthen him an angel from heaven appeared to him. He was in such agony and he prayed so fervently that his sweat became like drops of blood falling on the ground. When he rose from prayer and returned to his disciples, he found them sleeping from grief. He said to them, "Why are you sleeping? Get up and pray that you may not undergo the test."

While he was still speaking, a crowd approached and in front was one of the Twelve, a man named Judas. He went up to Jesus to kiss him. Jesus said to him, "Judas, are you betraying the Son of Man with a kiss?" His disciples realized what was about to happen, and they asked, "Lord, shall we strike with a sword?" And one of them struck the high priest's servant and cut off his right ear. But Jesus said in reply, "Stop, no more of this!" Then he touched the servant's ear and healed him. And Jesus said to the chief priests and temple guards and elders who had come for him, "Have you come out as against a robber, with swords and clubs? Day after day I was with you in the temple area, and you did not seize me; but this is your hour, the time for the power of darkness."

After arresting him they led him away and took him into the house of the high priest; Peter was following at a distance. They lit a fire in the middle of the courtyard and sat around it, and Peter sat down with them. When a maid saw him seated in the light, she looked intently at him and said, "This man too was with him." But he denied it saying, "Woman, I do not know him." A short while later someone else saw him and said, "You too are one of them"; but Peter answered, "My friend, I am not." About an hour later, still another insisted, "Assuredly, this man too was with him, for he also is a Galilean." But Peter said, "My friend, I do not know what you are talking about." Just as he was saying this, the cock crowed, and the Lord turned and looked at Peter; and Peter remembered the word of the Lord, how he had said to him, "Before the cock crows today, you will deny me three times." He went out and began to weep bitterly. The men who held Jesus in custody were ridiculing and beating him. They blindfolded him and questioned him, saying, "Prophesy! Who is it that struck you?" And they reviled him in saying many other things against him.

When day came the council of elders of the people met, both chief priests and scribes, and they brought him before their Sanhedrin. They said, "If you are the Christ, tell us," but he replied to them, "If I tell you, you will not believe, and if I question, you will not respond. But from this time on the Son of Man will be seated at the right hand of the power of God." They all asked, "Are you then the Son of God?" He replied to them, "You say that I am." Then they said, "What further need have we for testimony? We have heard it from his own mouth."

Then the whole assembly of them arose and brought him before Pilate. They brought charges against him, saying, "We found this man misleading our people; he opposes the payment of taxes to Caesar and maintains that he is the Christ, a king." Pilate asked him, "Are you the king of the Jews?" He said to him in reply, "You say so." Pilate then addressed the chief priests and the crowds, "I find this man not guilty." But they were adamant and said, "He is inciting the people with his teaching throughout all Judea, from Galilee where he began even to here."

On hearing this Pilate asked if the man was a Galilean; and upon learning that he was under Herod's jurisdiction, he sent him to Herod, who was in Jerusalem at that time. Herod was very glad to see Jesus; he had been wanting to see him for a long time, for he had heard about him and had been hoping to see him perform some sign. He questioned him at length, but he gave him no answer. The chief priests and scribes, meanwhile, stood by accusing him harshly. Herod and his soldiers treated him contemptuously and mocked him, and after clothing him in resplendent garb, he sent him back to Pilate. Herod and Pilate became friends that very day, even though they had been enemies formerly. Pilate then summoned the chief priests, the rulers, and the people and said to them, "You brought this man to me and accused him of inciting the people to revolt. I have conducted my investigation in your presence and have not found this man guilty of the charges you have brought against him, nor did Herod, for he sent him back to us. So no capital crime has been committed by him. Therefore I shall have him flogged and then release him."

But all together they shouted out, "Away with this man! Release Barabbas to us." —Now Barabbas had been imprisoned for a rebellion that had taken place in the city and for murder.— Again Pilate addressed them, still wishing to release Jesus, but they continued their shouting, "Crucify him! Crucify him!" Pilate addressed them a third time, "What evil has this man done? I found him guilty of no capital crime. Therefore I shall have him flogged and then release him." With loud shouts, however, they persisted in calling for his crucifixion, and their voices prevailed. The verdict of Pilate was that their demand should be granted. So he released the man who had been imprisoned for rebellion and murder, for whom they asked, and he handed Jesus over to them to deal with as they wished.

As they led him away they took hold of a certain Simon, a Cyrenian, who was coming in from the country; and after laying the cross on him, they made him carry it behind Jesus. A large crowd of people followed Jesus, including many women who mourned and lamented him.

Jesus turned to them and said, "Daughters of Jerusalem, do not weep for me; weep instead for yourselves and for your children for indeed, the days are coming when people will say, 'Blessed are the barren, the wombs that never bore and the breasts that never nursed.' At that time people will say to the mountains, 'Fall upon us!' and to the hills, 'Cover us!' for if these things are done when the wood is green, what will happen when it is dry?" Now two others, both criminals, were led away with him to be executed.

When they came to the place called the Skull, they crucified him and the criminals there, one on his right, the other on his left. Then Jesus said, "Father, forgive them, they know not what they do." They divided his garments by casting lots. The people stood by and watched; the rulers, meanwhile, sneered at him and said, "He saved others, let him save himself if he is the chosen one, the Christ of God." Even the soldiers jeered at him. As they approached to offer him wine they called out, "If you are King of the Jews, save yourself." Above him there was an inscription that read, "This is the King of the Jews."

Now one of the criminals hanging there reviled Jesus, saying, "Are you not the Christ? Save yourself and us." The other, however, rebuking him, said in reply, "Have you no fear of God, for you are subject to the same condemnation? And indeed, we have been condemned justly, for the sentence we received corresponds to our crimes, but this man has done nothing criminal." Then he said, "Jesus, remember me when you come into your kingdom." He replied to him, "Amen, I say to you, today you will be with me in Paradise."

It was now about noon and darkness came over the whole land until three in the afternoon because of an eclipse of the sun. Then the veil of the temple was torn down the middle. Jesus cried out in a loud voice, "Father, into your hands I commend my spirit"; and when he had said this he breathed his last.

Here all kneel and pause for a short time.

The centurion who witnessed what had happened glorified God and said, "This man was innocent beyond doubt." When all the people who had gathered for this spectacle saw what had happened, they returned home beating their breasts; but all his acquaintances stood at a distance, including the women who had followed him from Galilee and saw these events.

Now there was a virtuous and righteous man named Joseph, who, though he was a member of the council, had not consented to their plan of action. He came from the Jewish town of Arimathea and was awaiting the kingdom of God. He went to Pilate and asked for the body of Jesus. After he had taken the body down, he wrapped it in a linen cloth and laid him in a rock-hewn tomb in which no one had yet been buried. It was the day of preparation, and the sabbath was about to begin. The women who had come from Galilee with him followed behind, and when they had seen the tomb and the way in which his body was laid in it, they returned and prepared spices and perfumed oils. Then they rested on the sabbath according to the commandment.

LUKE 22: 14-71 & 23: 1-56

Shorter form: LUKE 23:1-49

ST. JOHN OF THE CROSS

Commenting on Baptism, John of the Cross completes his treatment of God's espousal of the soul by means of his Son's death.

"The espousal made on the cross is not the one we now speak of. For that espousal is accomplished immediately when God gives the first grace that is bestowed on each one at baptism. The espousal of which we speak bears reference to perfection and is not achieved save gradually and by stages. For though it is all one espousal, there is a difference in that one is

attained at the soul's pace, and thus little by little, and the other at God's pace, and thus immediately.

"*This espousal we are dealing with is what God makes known through Ezekiel by saying to the soul*: You were cast out upon the earth in contempt of your soul on the day you were born. And passing by you I saw you trodden under foot in your blood. And I said to you as you were in your blood: Love and be as multiplied as the grass of the field. Increase and grow great and enter and reach the stature of womanhood. And your breasts grew and your hair increased, and you were naked and full of confusion. And I passed by you and looked at you and saw that your time was the time of lovers, and I held my mantle over you and covered your ignominy. And I swore to you and entered into a pact with you and made you mine. And I washed you with water and cleansed the blood from you and anointed you with oil; and I clothed you in color and shod you with violet shoes, girded you with fine linen and clothed you with fine woven garments. And I adorned you with ornaments, put bracelets on your hands and a chain on your neck. And above your mouth I placed a ring, and I put earrings in your ears and a beautiful crown on your head. And you were adorned with gold and silver and clothed with fine linen and embroidered silk and many colors. You ate very choice bread and honey and oil, and you became exceedingly beautiful, and advanced to rule and be a queen. And your name was spread among the people because of your beauty [Ez 16:5–14]. *These are the words of Ezekiel. And so it happens with the soul of which we are speaking*"(C 23.6).

REFLECTION

Like the Gospels, the Season of Lent converges on the Passion Narrative of our Lord Jesus Christ. Each Gospel has its own theological outlook on the event. For Luke, the theological reason for Jesus' suffering and death in obedience to the Father's will was done, as in Mark, for the promotion of the Kingdom of God. However, unlike Mark, Luke adds that the Kingdom of God is the way of service to one another: *"Then an argument broke out among them about which of them should be regarded as the greatest. He said to them, The kings of the Gentiles lord it over them and those in authority over them are addressed as 'Benefactors'; but among you it shall not be so. Rather, let the greatest among you be as the youngest, and the leader as the servant. For who is greater: the one seated at table or the one who serves? Is it not the one seated at table? I am among you as the one who serves* [Lk 22:24–27]."

For John of the Cross, the theological perspective is espousal. It is not the vision of Luke, but it is out of this experience of the soul's espousal to God through Christ that the soul will be able to live a life of service to her brothers and sisters as Jesus desired. The soul, having been freed from pride, self-love, and self-seeking, becomes a truly humble soul available for service.

PRAYER

God, our Father, at our Baptism you renewed the work of your Son's death on the Cross in us, so that we could be his brothers and sisters as our Firstborn Brother and, as a consequence, your sons and daughters through him. Grant, we ask, that as we follow your Son through Passion Week, we may remember the great work you achieved in and for us in making us heirs through your Son. May we express our gratitude by keeping your commandment of love and embracing with faith, hope, and charity the crosses you send our way. We ask this through Christ your Son and our Lord. Amen.

GOSPEL

Six days before Passover Jesus came to Bethany, where Lazarus was, whom Jesus had raised from the dead. They gave a dinner for him there, and Martha served, while Lazarus was one of those reclining at table with him. Mary took a liter of costly perfumed oil made from genuine aromatic nard and anointed the feet of Jesus and dried them with her hair; the house was filled with the fragrance of the oil. Then Judas the Iscariot, one of his disciples, and the one who would betray him, said, "Why was this oil not sold for three hundred days' wages and given to the poor?" He said this not because he cared about the poor but because he was a thief and held the money bag and used to steal the contributions. So Jesus said, "Leave her alone. Let her keep this for the day of my burial. You always have the poor with you, but you do not always have me."

The large crowd of the Jews found out that he was there and came, not only because of him, but also to see Lazarus, whom he had raised from the dead. And the chief priests plotted to kill Lazarus too, because many of the Jews were turning away and believing in Jesus because of him.

JOHN 12: 1-11

ST. JOHN OF THE CROSS

St. John of the Cross describes a soul dedicated to loving God in the same way that Mary loves God.

"Aware of the Bridegroom's words in the Gospel, that no one can serve two masters but must necessarily fail one [Mt 6:24], the soul claims here that in order not to fail God she failed all that is not God, that is, herself and all other creatures, losing all these for love of him.

"Anyone truly in love will let all other things go in order to come closer to the loved one. On this account the soul affirms here that she lost herself. She achieved this in two ways: she became lost to herself by paying no attention to herself in anything, by concentrating on her Beloved and surrendering herself to him freely and disinterestedly, with no desire to gain anything for herself; second, she became lost to all creatures, paying no heed to all her own affairs but only to those of her Beloved. And this is to love herself purposely, which is to desire to be found.

"The one who walks in the love of God seeks neither gain nor reward, but seeks only to lose with the will all things and self for God; and this loss the lover judges to be a gain. Thus it is, as St. Paul asserts: Mori lucrum [Phil 1:21], *that is, my death for Christ is my gain, spiritually, of all things and of myself. Consequently the soul declares: I was found. The soul that does not know how to lose herself does not find herself but rather loses herself, as Our Lord teaches in the Gospel:* Those who desire to gain their soul shall lose it, and those who lose it for my sake shall gain it [Mt 16:25].

"Should we desire to interpret this verse more spiritually and in closer accord with what we are discussing here, it ought to be known that when a soul treading the spiritual road has reached such a point that she has lost all roads and natural methods in her communion with God, and no longer seeks him by reflections or forms or feelings or by any other way of creatures and the senses, but has advanced beyond them all and beyond all modes and manners, and enjoys communion with God in faith and love, then it is said that God is her gain, because she has certainly lost all that is not God" (C 29.10–11).

REFLECTION

In today's Gospel passage Martha's sister, Mary, spent lavishly on Jesus by pouring an expensive oil over the feet of Jesus. She did this with no concern for her reputation or the approval of others. She did it entirely out of love for Jesus. Jesus appreciated this gesture not so much for it having been done to himself but because he saw in it Mary's total gift of self, a gift that was not preoccupied with herself but with Jesus.

John of the Cross similarly describes a soul who has become totally lost to self-preoccupation and totally found with regard to God. We live in a world where we are encouraged to be preoccupied with our health, our wealth, our future of how we will spend our last years, and so forth. All these are to a certain extent necessary; but it could be wondered how free are we to remember God when we become totally absorbed in our own needs?

John of the Cross describes a soul who has failed in everything that did not concern God. Such a soul had earlier become possessed by God, or at least drawn by God to free herself from all about herself that did not concern God as John of the Cross says in his Ascent:

"The soul, then, states that 'fired with love's urgent longings' it passed through this night of sense to union with the Beloved. A love of pleasure, and attachment to it, usually fires the will toward the enjoyment of things that give pleasure. <u>A more intense enkindling of another, better love (love of the soul's Bridegroom) is necessary for the vanquishing of the appetites and the denial of this pleasure.</u> By finding satisfaction and strength in this love, it will have the courage and constancy to readily deny all other appetites. The love of its Bridegroom is not the only requisite for conquering the strength of the sensitive appetites; an enkindling with urgent longings of love is also necessary. For the sensory appetites are moved and attracted toward sensory objects with such cravings that if the spiritual part of the soul is not fired with other, more urgent longings for spiritual things, the soul will be able neither to overcome the yoke of nature nor to enter the

night of sense; nor will it have the courage to live in the darkness of all things by denying its appetites for them [emphasis my own]" (A 1.14.2).

At some point in Mary's life, Jesus enkindled in her a love for him that enabled her to forget herself and remember only Jesus. How this happens for each one of us will be different; but fidelity to the Lenten practices of prayer, fasting, and almsgiving do open the door, even if ever so slightly, to become enamored by the love of God, to make greater acts of self-forgetfulness and being habitually mindful of God and all that concerns God. Blessed are they who have begun.

PRAYER

Lord God, in the example of Mary at Bethany, you showed an example of disinterested love for your Son. Grant, we ask, that we too may love your Son with the same disinterested love and express it by dying to our self-seeking and self-loving through the sufferings you send us. We ask this through Christ our Lord. Amen.

GOSPEL

Reclining at table with his disciples, Jesus was deeply troubled and testified, "Amen, amen, I say to you, one of you will betray me." The disciples looked at one another, at a loss as to whom he meant. One of his disciples, the one whom Jesus loved, was reclining at Jesus' side. So Simon Peter nodded to him to find out whom he meant. He leaned back against Jesus' chest and said to him, "Master, who is it?" Jesus answered, "It is the one to whom I hand the morsel after I have dipped it." So he dipped the morsel and took it and handed it to Judas, son of Simon the Iscariot. After Judas took the morsel, Satan entered him. So Jesus said to him, "What you are going to do, do quickly." Now none of those reclining at table realized why he said this to him. Some thought that since Judas kept the money bag, Jesus had told him, "Buy what we need for the feast," or to give something to the poor. So Judas took the morsel and left at once. And it was night.

When he had left, Jesus said, "Now is the Son of Man glorified, and God is glorified in him. If God is glorified in him, God will also glorify him in himself, and he will glorify him at once. My children, I will be with you only a little while longer. You will look for me, and as I told the Jews, 'Where I go you cannot come,' so now I say it to you."

Simon Peter said to him, "Master, where are you going?" Jesus answered him, "Where I am going, you cannot follow me now, though you will follow later." Peter said to him, "Master, why can I not follow you now? I will lay down my life for you." Jesus answered, "Will you lay down your life for me? Amen, amen, I say to you, the cock will not crow before you deny me three times."

JOHN 13: 21-33, 36-38

ST. JOHN OF THE CROSS

John of the Cross portrays the vice that brought about Judas' downfall, avariciousness.

"The fourth degree of this privative harm is noted in the final statement of the text: and departed from God his Savior [Dt 32:15]. *This is the degree into which the avaricious ones we just mentioned fall. Because of temporal goods, the avaricious do not concern themselves with setting their heart on God's law, and consequently their will, memory, and intellect wander far from God and they forget him, as though he were not their God at all. The reason is that they have made gods for themselves out of money and temporal goods. St. Paul indicates this in declaring that avarice is a form of idolatry* [Col. 3:5]. *Those who are in this fourth degree forget God and deliberately turn their heart—which ought to be centered on him—to money, as though they had no other God"* (A 3.19.8).

REFLECTION

The betrayal of Jesus by Judas is a sobering memory for Christians. How could one who ate and drank with Jesus, saw his miracles, and ministered with or for him betray his Lord? The Gospel of John simply says that Judas did so for the love of money. St. John of the Cross writes that those who live to possess things are those who by degrees forget God and this is because they have made possessions their god.

During the Season of Lent we strive to overcome this vice of having and seeking possessions through the work of almsgiving. Through almsgiving, we create a balance against our desire to have and possess things. When we look at our acts of charity through almsgiving, as though they were separated from other concerns, they seem merely acts of simple charity; but as we can see in the example of Judas and in the teaching of John of the Cross, these acts may have a much greater significance. They can save us from living as though Christ did not die and free us from our selfishness.

PRAYER

Lord, God, through the Season of Lent, you taught us to find our true treasure in Jesus your Son by the practices of prayer, fasting, and almsgiving. Grant, we ask, that, as we follow your Son throughout Holy Week, we may imitate his abandonment to you and not become seduced by the world's goods as the apostle who betrayed him did. We ask this in Jesus, your Son's name. Amen.

GOSPEL

One of the Twelve, who was called Judas Iscariot, went to the chief priests and said, "What are you willing to give me if I hand him over to you?" They paid him thirty pieces of silver, and from that time on he looked for an opportunity to hand him over.

On the first day of the Feast of Unleavened Bread, the disciples approached Jesus and said, "Where do you want us to prepare for you to eat the Passover?" He said, "Go into the city to a certain man and tell him, 'The teacher says, My appointed time draws near; in your house I shall celebrate the Passover with my disciples.'" The disciples then did as Jesus had ordered, and prepared the Passover.

When it was evening, he reclined at table with the Twelve. And while they were eating, he said, "Amen, I say to you, one of you will betray me." Deeply distressed at this, they began to say to him one after another, "Surely it is not I, Lord?" He said in reply, "He who has dipped his hand into the dish with me is the one who will betray me. The Son of Man indeed goes, as it is written of him, but woe to that man by whom the Son of Man is betrayed. It would be better for that man if he had never been born." Then Judas, his betrayer, said in reply, "Surely it is not I, Rabbi?" He answered, "You have said so."

MATTHEW 26: 14-25

ST. JOHN OF THE CROSS

We saw this text on Tuesday of the Fourth Week of Lent. It is repeated here because Jesus is betrayed by one of his followers. This betrayal will lead Jesus into his dark night of feeling abandoned by all, including his Father.

"Such persons also feel forsaken and despised by creatures, particularly by

their friends. David immediately adds: You have withdrawn my friends and acquaintances far from me; they have considered me an abomination [Ps 88:8]. *Jonah, as one who also underwent this experience, both physically and spiritually in the belly of the whale, testifies:* You have cast me out into the deep, into the heart of the sea, and the current surrounded me; all its whirlpools and waves passed over me and I said: I am cast from the sight of your eyes; yet I shall see your holy temple again (he says this because God purifies the soul that it might see his temple); the waters encircled me even to the soul, the abyss went round about me, the open sea covered my head, I descended to the lowest parts of the mountains, the locks of the earth closed me up forever [Jon. 2:4–7]. *The 'locks' refer to the soul's imperfections that hinder it from enjoying the delights of this contemplation"* (N 2.6.3).

REFLECTION

Probably one of the hardest experiences we will ever undergo in our lives is to be betrayed by a friend. When it happens, we feel confused, stunned, and hurt. How could the one we had placed so much trust in let me down at a time like this? is a question that many of us ask during such times. Jesus too knew of this experience of being betrayed by one of those he had called to follow him; and when Judas had left, Jesus was plunged into a dark night, where he was to experience the abandonment of his friends, his people, and even his God.

When we undergo like experiences, there are no words to comfort us. John of the Cross says not to trouble such people because they are beyond the consolation of words. The best one could do is to be present and as supportive as one can.

While the way out for an immediate relief seems closed, John of the Cross, sees a lot of good coming from such experiences. This is because he sees that through this experience of the dark night, the soul grows in its capacity to see God's temple and thus, be able to live in God's presence.

For John of the Cross, there is always more to God because God cannot be contained by the limits of our own understanding nor the limits of our own unredeemed hearts. As a result, God needs to stretch us through suffering so that we may be able to grow in our capactity to experience him.

As we follow Christ in the dark night of his passion, may we draw strength from his example to remain faithful to him when we undergo the same.

PRAYER

Lord God, your Son saw in the betrayal of his apostle the beginning of that suffering that would lead to his death on the Cross. Grant, we ask, that we may remain loyal to him and to you when all else fails, and so merit to be true brothers and sisters in the example of Christ our Lord. We ask this in his name. Amen.

PASCHAL
TRIDUUM

GOSPEL

Jesus came to Nazareth, where he had grown up, and went according to his custom into the synagogue on the sabbath day. He stood up to read and was handed a scroll of the prophet Isaiah. He unrolled the scroll and found the passage where it was written:

The Spirit of the Lord is upon me,
because he has anointed me
    to bring glad tidings to the poor.
He has sent me to proclaim liberty to captives
    and recovery of sight to the blind,
    to let the oppressed go free,
and to proclaim a year acceptable to the Lord.

Rolling up the scroll, he handed it back to the attendant and sat down, and the eyes of all in the synagogue looked intently at him. He said to them, "Today this Scripture passage is fulfilled in your hearing."

LUKE 4: 16-21

ST. JOHN OF THE CROSS

Along with writing about what we must do to attain union with God, John of the Cross writes about how God anoints souls to prepare them for union with him.

"During this time of the betrothal and expectation of marriage and the anointings of the Holy Spirit, when the ointments preparatory for union

---

† The Chrism Mass is the annual Mass when the bishop blesses the oils that will be used for the sacraments throughout the year in the diocese.

with God are more sublime, the anxieties of the caverns of the soul are usually extreme and delicate. Since these ointments are a more proximate preparation for union with God (for they are more closely related to God and consequently lure the soul and make it relish him more delicately), the desire for him becomes more refined and profound—and the desire for God is the preparation for union with him.

"In the first place it should be known that if anyone is seeking God, the Beloved is seeking that person much more. And if a soul directs to God its loving desires, which are as fragrant to him as the pillar of smoke rising from the aromatic spices of myrrh and incense [Sg 3:6], God sends it the fragrance of his ointments by which he draws it and makes it run after him [Sg 1:3], and these are his divine inspirations and touches. As often as these inspirations and touches are his, they are always bound and regulated by the perfection of his law and of faith. It is by means of this perfection that a person must always draw closer to him. Thus it should be understood that the desire for himself that God grants in all his favors of unguents and fragrant anointings is a preparation for other more precious and delicate ointments, made more according to the quality of God, until the soul is so delicately and purely prepared that it merits union with him and substantial transformation in all its faculties" (F 3.26, 28).

REFLECTION

A question we can ask ourselves is: what do I do today to draw another person's attention to me, to my love for that person, for that person to know that I care for him or her in a special way? In our culture this act usually takes the form of a gift. It is usually wrapped in fine or colorful paper and takes a little work to unwrap and possess.

What we do for one another in trying to draw the other's attention to our love, God does to us. For John of the Cross, God sends us experiences of his presence that awakens us to his love. The more we give ourselves to these touches or anointings of his love the more we desire him and direct our energies toward him. In the end, God and the soul become one in their mutual effort to direct their energies toward one another. Another way of understanding this is to see God and the soul as having a synergy love for one another: the energy of the one inviting and enlivening the energy of the other, as they become more and more intensely united with one another.

In today's Gospel, we hear the prophet proclaiming the Lord's spirit is upon him because the Lord has anointed him. The Lord thus made him Messiah or the Anointed One. The word Christ comes from the Greek word for anointing and as Jesus was anointed by God, he has been called Christ.

We, who are Christians, are anointed several times in our lives: at Baptism, at Confirmation, and when we receive the Sacrament of the Sick. Those who are called to the priesthood receive another kind of anointing of the hands to prepare them for their ministry. While all these anointings have different ends in mind, they all serve as a reminder that God loves us and has united us to himself in his family, founded on the one he had anointed, Jesus of Nazareth.

PRAYER

Lord God, at our Baptism you anointed us to partake in the royal priesthood of your Son through your minister and at our Confirmation you anointed us with the seal of the Holy Spirit through your bishop. Grant, we ask, that through these anointings, we may partake ever more fully in the divine life your Son merited for us in his suffering and death on the Cross. We ask this through Christ, our Lord. Amen.

GOSPEL

Before the feast of Passover, Jesus knew that his hour had come to pass from this world to the Father. He loved his own in the world and he loved them to the end. The devil had already induced Judas, son of Simon the Iscariot, to hand him over. So, during supper, fully aware that the Father had put everything into his power and that he had come from God and was returning to God, he rose from supper and took off his outer garments. He took a towel and tied it around his waist. Then he poured water into a basin and began to wash the disciples' feet and dry them with the towel around his waist. He came to Simon Peter, who said to him, "Master, are you going to wash my feet?" Jesus answered and said to him, "What I am doing, you do not understand now, but you will understand later." Peter said to him, "You will never wash my feet." Jesus answered him, "Unless I wash you, you will have no inheritance with me." Simon Peter said to him, "Master, then not only my feet, but my hands and head as well." Jesus said to him, "Whoever has bathed has no need except to have his feet washed, for he is clean all over; so you are clean, but not all." For he knew who would betray him; for this reason, he said, "Not all of you are clean."

So when he had washed their feet and put his garments back on and reclined at table again, he said to them, "Do you realize what I have done for you? You call me 'teacher' and 'master,' and rightly so, for indeed I am. If I, therefore, the master and teacher, have washed your feet, you ought to wash one another's feet. I have given you a model to follow, so that as I have done for you, you should also do."

JOHN 13: 1-15

ST. JOHN OF THE CROSS

John of the Cross defends those called to serve Christ by remaining in his presence.

"The soul, indeed, lost to all things and won over to love, no longer occupies her spirit in anything else. She even withdraws in matters pertinent to the active life and other exterior exercises for the sake of fulfilling the one thing the Bridegroom said was necessary [Lk 10:42], and that is: attentiveness to God and the continual exercise of love in him. This the Lord values and esteems so highly that he reproved Martha when she tried to call Mary away from her place at his feet in order to busy her with other active things in his service; and Martha thought that she herself was doing all the work and Mary, because she was enjoying the Lord's presence, was doing nothing [Lk. 10:39–41]. Yet, since there is no greater or more necessary work than love, the contrary is true. The Lord also defends the bride in the Song of Songs, conjuring all creatures of the world, referred to by the daughters of Jerusalem, not to hinder the bride's spiritual sleep of love or cause her to awaken or open her eyes to anything else until she desire [Sg3:5].

"It should be noted that until the soul reaches this state of union of love, she should practice love in both the active and contemplative life. Yet once she arrives she should not become involved in other works and exterior exercises that might be of the slightest hindrance to the attentiveness of love toward God, even though the work be of great service to God. For a little of this pure love is more precious to God and the soul and more beneficial to the Church, even though it seems one is doing nothing, than all these other works put together.

"Because of her determined desire to please her Bridegroom and benefit the Church, Mary Magdalene, even though she was accomplishing great good by her preaching and would have continued doing so, hid in the desert for 30 years in order to surrender herself truly to this love. It seemed to her, after all, that by such retirement she would obtain much more because of the notable benefit and gain that a little of this love brings to the Church" (C 29.1–2).

REFLECTION

In his book On Love, Joseph Piper wrote that love is an act in which one person says to another, "It is good that you are." In this phrase, the speaker tells his listener that his goodness is not based on any attribute or accomplishment but on the simple fact of his existence. When Jesus washed the feet of his disciples, he was telling them, in effect, that it was good that they were, that they existed, apart from whether they could understand his deed or not, or later support him or betray him. He was telling them that it was good that they were.

To a certain extent, he was doing one step better. This was because in his day, there were no shoes and as a result a person's feet got dirty along the way by everything that fell onto the roads. By cleaning their feet, Jesus was bringing them back to their original goodness, the goodness they had before the roads of life made them dirty, and by implication, sinful in the eyes of God. Jesus was saying in effect: "I can make you graceful in the eyes of God again." He offered them an opportunity to find their original goodness in this very humble and servile act.[1]

Jesus also affirmed his Father. In chapter 17 of the Gospel of John, he told the Father that it was good that he was as he was in the beginning before the creation of the world, as he was then, and will be forever. The word that Jesus used to describe the Father's goodness was *glory*. Glory is such a basic aspect of God that it cannot be considered an attribute. In this prayer, Jesus asked to be given this glory that he had before the world was created; and he asked that it be given to his followers as well, so that they could share in his life with the Father.

You might say that the Gospel of John is a testament to Jesus finding goodness in all people: whether it be the Samaritan woman, the woman caught in adultery, the man born blind, or the man by the pool waiting for someone to help him get in, all discovered their basic good-

---

1. See John J. Pilch, *The Triduum and Easter Sunday: Breaking Open the Scriptures,* (Collegeville, MN: The Liturgical Press, 2000), 8.

ness and reality that they were lovable in God's eyes.

After his Resurrection, Jesus called his disciples to continue his mission of revealing the goodness each person was created with by God as he did with Peter when he commanded him to feed his sheep three times. He left room for some to focus on God's love exclusively as he did with the beloved disciple whose only tasks were to care for Jesus' mother and wait for his return. You might say that in the Church of John's Gospel there are two major charisms: to feed the Lord's sheep, and to await his return in glory. Both make up the Church and contribute to her growth in holiness.

John of the Cross focused on the latter because it was as rare in his day as it is in our's and it is much more difficult to live. It is easier to explain the former as a form of doing while the latter is a form of being. Still, it must be remembered that for John of the Cross both are forms of loving, both tell God either in works, or in contemplation, that "It is good that you are." Both involve acts of selflessness and self-emptying love in order to partake in God's selfless and self-emptying love in his Son's Incarnation and Crucifixion.

May our traveling with the Lord at his Last Meal with his disciples enable us to see God's love for the goodness he has created in us and enable us to share it with others in deeds and prayer.

PRAYER

Lord, God, in your Son's divestment of his garments to wash the feet of his disciples, you gave us an example of unselfish love in the service of our brothers and sisters. Grant, we ask, that we may practice this same unselfish act of love in our own lives, whether we be in prayer or in service. We ask this through Christ, our Lord. Amen.

GOSPEL

Jesus went out with his disciples across the Kidron valley to where there was a garden, into which he and his disciples entered. Judas his betrayer also knew the place, because Jesus had often met there with his disciples. So Judas got a band of soldiers and guards from the chief priests and the Pharisees and went there with lanterns, torches, and weapons. Jesus, knowing everything that was going to happen to him, went out and said to them, "Whom are you looking for?" They answered him, "Jesus the Nazorean." He said to them, "I AM." Judas his betrayer was also with them. When he said to them, "I AM," they turned away and fell to the ground. So he again asked them, "Whom are you looking for?" They said, "Jesus the Nazorean." Jesus answered, "I told you that I AM. So if you are looking for me, let these men go." This was to fulfill what he had said, "I have not lost any of those you gave me." Then Simon Peter, who had a sword, drew it, struck the high priest's slave, and cut off his right ear. The slave's name was Malchus. Jesus said to Peter, "Put your sword into its scabbard. Shall I not drink the cup that the Father gave me?"

So the band of soldiers, the tribune, and the Jewish guards seized Jesus, bound him, and brought him to Annas first. He was the father-in-law of Caiaphas, who was high priest that year. It was Caiaphas who had counseled the Jews that it was better that one man should die rather than the people.

Simon Peter and another disciple followed Jesus. Now the other disciple was known to the high priest, and he entered the courtyard of the high priest with Jesus. But Peter stood at the gate outside. So the other disciple, the acquaintance of the high priest, went out and spoke to the gatekeeper and brought Peter in. Then the maid who was the gatekeeper said to Peter, "You are not one of this man's disciples, are you?" He said, "I am not." Now the slaves and the guards were standing around a charcoal fire that they had made, because it was cold, and were warming themselves. Peter was also standing there keeping warm.

The high priest questioned Jesus about his disciples and about his doctrine. Jesus answered him, "I have spoken publicly to the world. I have always taught in a synagogue or in the temple area where all the Jews gather, and in secret I have said nothing. Why ask me? Ask those who heard me what I said to them. They know what I said." When he had said this, one of the temple guards standing there struck Jesus and said, "Is this the way you answer the high priest?" Jesus answered him, "If I have spoken wrongly, testify to the wrong; but if I have spoken rightly, why do you strike me?" Then Annas sent him bound to Caiaphas the high priest.

Now Simon Peter was standing there keeping warm. And they said to him, "You are not one of his disciples, are you?" He denied it and said, "I am not." One of the slaves of the high priest, a relative of the one whose ear Peter had cut off, said, "Didn't I see you in the garden with him?" Again Peter denied it. And immediately the cock crowed.

Then they brought Jesus from Caiaphas to the praetorium. It was morning. And they themselves did not enter the praetorium, in order not to be defiled so that they could eat the Passover. So Pilate came out to them and said, "What charge do you bring against this man?" They answered and said to him, "If he were not a criminal, we would not have handed him over to you." At this, Pilate said to them, "Take him yourselves, and judge him according to your law." The Jews answered him, "We do not have the right to execute anyone," in order that the word of Jesus might be fulfilled that he said indicating the kind of death he would die.

So Pilate went back into the praetorium and summoned Jesus and said to him, "Are you the King of the Jews?" Jesus answered, "Do you say this on your own or have others told you about me?" Pilate answered, "I am not a Jew, am I? Your own nation and the chief priests handed you over to me. What have you done?" Jesus answered, "My kingdom does not belong to this world. If my kingdom did belong to this world, my attendants would be fighting to keep me from being handed over to the Jews. But as it is, my kingdom is not here." So Pilate said to him, "Then you are a king?" Jesus answered, "You say I am a king. For this I was born and for this I came into the world, to testify to the truth. Everyone who belongs to the truth listens to my voice." Pilate said to him, "What is truth?"

When he had said this, he again went out to the Jews and said to them, "I find no guilt in him. But you have a custom that I release one prisoner to you at Passover. Do you want me to release to you the King of the Jews?" They cried out again, "Not this one but Barabbas!" Now Barabbas was a revolutionary.

Then Pilate took Jesus and had him scourged. And the soldiers wove a crown out of thorns and placed it on his head, and clothed him in a purple cloak, and they came to him and said, "Hail, King of the Jews!" And they struck him repeatedly. Once more Pilate went out and said to them, "Look, I am bringing him out to you, so that you may know that I find no guilt in him." So Jesus came out, wearing the crown of thorns and the purple cloak. And he said to them, "Behold, the man!" When the chief priests and the guards saw him they cried out, "Crucify him, crucify him!" Pilate said to them, "Take him yourselves and crucify him. I find no guilt in him." The Jews answered, "We have a law, and according to that law he ought to die, because he made himself the Son of God." Now when Pilate heard this statement, he became even more afraid, and went back into the praetorium and said to Jesus, "Where are you from?" Jesus did not answer him. So Pilate said to him, "Do you not speak to me? Do you not know that I have power to release you and I have power to crucify you?" Jesus answered him, "You would have no power over me if it had not been given to you from above. For this reason the one who handed me over to you has the greater sin." Consequently, Pilate tried to release him;

but the Jews cried out, "If you release him, you are not a Friend of Caesar. Everyone who makes himself a king opposes Caesar."

When Pilate heard these words he brought Jesus out and seated him on the judge's bench in the place called Stone Pavement, in Hebrew, Gabbatha. It was preparation day for Passover, and it was about noon. And he said to the Jews, "Behold, your king!" They cried out, "Take him away, take him away! Crucify him!" Pilate said to them, "Shall I crucify your king?" The chief priests answered, "We have no king but Caesar." Then he handed him over to them to be crucified.

So they took Jesus, and, carrying the cross himself, he went out to what is called the Place of the Skull, in Hebrew, Golgotha. There they crucified him, and with him two others, one on either side, with Jesus in the middle. Pilate also had an inscription written and put on the cross. It read, "Jesus the Nazorean, the King of the Jews." Now many of the Jews read this inscription, because the place where Jesus was crucified was near the city; and it was written in Hebrew, Latin, and Greek. So the chief priests of the Jews said to Pilate, "Do not write 'The King of the Jews,' but that he said, 'I am the King of the Jews'." Pilate answered, "What I have written, I have written."

When the soldiers had crucified Jesus, they took his clothes and divided them into four shares, a share for each soldier. They also took his tunic, but the tunic was seamless, woven in one piece from the top down. So they said to one another, "Let's not tear it, but cast lots for it to see whose it will be," in order that the passage of Scripture might be fulfilled that says:

They divided my garments among them,
and for my vesture they cast lots.

This is what the soldiers did. Standing by the cross of Jesus were his mother and his mother's sister, Mary the wife of Clopas, and Mary of Magdala. When Jesus saw his mother and the disciple there whom he loved he said to his mother, "Woman, behold, your son." Then he said to the disciple, "Behold, your mother." And from that hour the disciple took her into his home.

After this, aware that everything was now finished, in order that the Scripture might be fulfilled, Jesus said, "I thirst." There was a vessel filled with common wine. So they put a sponge soaked in wine on a sprig of hyssop and put it up to his mouth. When Jesus had taken the wine, he said, "It is finished." And bowing his head, he handed over the spirit.

Here all kneel and pause for a short time.

Now since it was preparation day, in order that the bodies might not remain on the cross on the sabbath, for the sabbath day of that week was a solemn one, the Jews asked Pilate that their legs be broken and that they be taken down. So the soldiers came and broke the legs of the first and then of the other one who was crucified with Jesus. But when they came to Jesus and saw that he was already dead, they did not break his legs, but one soldier thrust his lance into his side, and immediately blood and water flowed out. An eyewitness has testified, and his testimony is true; he knows that he is speaking the truth, so that you also may come to believe. For this happened so that the Scripture passage might be fulfilled: *Not a bone of it will be broken.* And again another passage says: *They will look upon him whom they have pierced.*

After this, Joseph of Arimathea, secretly a disciple of Jesus for fear of the Jews, asked Pilate if he could remove the body of Jesus. And Pilate permitted it. So he came and took his body. Nicodemus, the one who had first come to him at night, also came bringing a mixture of myrrh and aloes weighing about one hundred pounds. They took the body of Jesus and bound it with burial cloths along with the spices, according to the Jewish burial custom. Now in the place where he had been crucified there was a garden, and in the garden a new tomb, in which no one had yet been buried. So they laid Jesus there because of the Jewish preparation day; for the tomb was close by.

JOHN 18: 1-40 & 19: 1-42

ST. JOHN OF THE CROSS

We saw this text on Monday of the Third Week of Lent. This time it is presented in the light of Jesus' actual crucifixion.

"Because I have said that Christ is the way and that this way is a death to our natural selves in the sensory and spiritual parts of the soul, I would like to demonstrate how this death is patterned on Christ's, for he is our model and light.

"First, during his life he certainly died spiritually to the sensitive part, and at his death he died naturally. He proclaimed during his life that he had no place whereon to lay his head [Mt 8:20]. And at his death he had less.

"Second, at the moment of his death he was certainly annihilated in his soul, without any consolation or relief, since the Father had left him that way in innermost aridity in the lower part. He was thereby compelled to cry out: My God, My God, why have you forsaken me? *[Mt 27:46]. This was the most extreme abandonment, sensitively, that he had suffered in his life. And by it he accomplished the most marvelous work of his whole life, surpassing all the works and deeds and miracles that he had ever performed on earth or in heaven. That is, he brought about the reconciliation and union of the human race with God through grace. The Lord achieved this, as I say, at the moment in which he was most annihilated in all things: in his reputation before people, since in watching him die they mocked him instead of esteeming him; in his human*

nature, by dying; and in spiritual help and consolation from his Father, for he was forsaken by his Father at that time, annihilated and reduced to nothing, so as to pay the debt fully and bring people to union with God. David says of him: Ad nihilum redactus sum et nescivi [Ps. 73:22] "I am brought to nothing, and I knew not," *that those who are truly spiritual might understand the mystery of the door and way (which is Christ) leading to union with God, and that they might realize that their union with God and the greatness of the work they accomplish will be measured by their annihilation of themselves for God in the sensory and spiritual parts of their souls. When they are reduced to nothing, the highest degree of humility, the spiritual union between their souls and God will be an accomplished fact. This union is the most noble and sublime state attainable in this life. The journey, then, does not consist in consolations, delights, and spiritual feelings, but in the living death of the cross, sensory and spiritual, exterior and interior"* (A 2.7.9–11).

REFLECTION

When Jesus had died on the Cross his dark night came to an end. When did his dark night began is hard to say. Certainly, it was apparent at the Garden of Gethsemene. There was his betrayal by Judas; but even before then Jesus was persecuted by his own after he healed the man who could not make it to the pool because others got in front of him (Jn 5:1–16). Whenever this dark night for Jesus began, it affected him in his most intimate center. When this happens to us, it feels as though death would be a relief from the constant torment, a torment that cannot be reasoned away nor consoled by a dear friend or counselor. This was something like Jesus underwent in his dark night.

From an empirical point of view, Jesus' suffering and death were no different from that of any other person's suffering and death. His death may have been provoked by him, the crowds, or just simply a mistake. In any case, it was just another human being's suffering and death.

From the point of view of faith, Jesus' suffering and death is the fulfillment of scripture, of God's plan for his Son and the human race. For John the Evangelist, Jesus' death was not a simple death of a man, but a triumph of the Son of God planned by God. For John of the Cross, Jesus' death achieved the reconciliation between God and the human race.

Whether you see in Jesus' death a victory over the world planned by God the Father; or, the reconciliation and union of the human race with God through grace, you are seeing the event of Jesus' death through the eyes of faith. This faith comes to us at Baptism and grows stronger or weaker as we invest our life in the reality of Jesus in deeds such as prayer, fasting, almsgiving, and accepting the crosses our own life hands us with faith, hope and love. God has given us the grace to see Jesus' death as salvific but he does not force it upon us to develop that grace. That he leaves to our freedom and our desire to be renewed in being born anew as children of God as John in his Gospel says: *"But to those who did accept him he gave power to become children of God, to those who believe in his name, who were born not by natural generation nor by human choice nor by a man's decision but of God"* [Jn 1:12].

PRAYER

Lord Jesus, to merit our return to communion with God, our Father, you accepted being emptied for our sake at your Incarnation and again at your Crucifixion. Grant, we ask, that we too may accept those crosses of our self-emptying in imitation of you and in order to participate in the divine life you have merited for us. We ask this in your name. Amen.

GOSPEL

After the sabbath, as the first day of the week was dawning, Mary Magdalene and the other Mary came to see the tomb. And behold, there was a great earthquake; for an angel of the Lord descended from heaven, approached, rolled back the stone, and sat upon it. His appearance was like lightning and his clothing was white as snow. The guards were shaken with fear of him and became like dead men. Then the angel said to the women in reply, "Do not be afraid! I know that you are seeking Jesus the crucified. He is not here, for he has been raised just as he said. Come and see the place where he lay. Then go quickly and tell his disciples, 'He has been raised from the dead, and he is going before you to Galilee; there you will see him.' Behold, I have told you." Then they went away quickly from the tomb, fearful yet overjoyed, and ran to announce this to his disciples. And behold, Jesus met them on their way and greeted them. They approached, embraced his feet, and did him homage. Then Jesus said to them, "Do not be afraid. Go tell my brothers to go to Galilee, and there they will see me."

MATTHEW 28: 1-10

ST. JOHN OF THE CROSS

Here John of the Cross writes about the Resurrection in the context of creation.

"St. Paul says: the Son of God is the splendor of his glory and the image of his substance [Heb 1:3]. *It should be known that only with this figure, his Son, did God look at all things, that is, he communicated to them their natural being and many natural graces and gifts, and made them complete and perfect, as is said in Genesis:* God looked at all things that he made, and they were very good [Gn 1:31]. *To look and behold that they were very good was to make them very good in the Word, his Son.*

"Not only by looking at them did he communicate natural being and graces, as we said, but also, with this image of his Son alone, he clothed them in beauty by imparting to them supernatural being. This he did when he took on our human nature and elevated it in the beauty of God, and consequently all creatures, since in human nature he was united with them all. Accordingly, the Son of God proclaimed: Si ego exaltatus a terra fuero omnia traham ad me ipsum (If I be lifted up from the earth, I will elevate all things to myself) [Jn 12:32]. *And in this elevation of all things through the Incarnation of his Son and through the glory of his resurrection according to the flesh not only did the Father beautify creatures partially, but, we can say, he clothed them entirely in beauty and dignity"* (C 5.4).

REFLECTION

This Vigil's Gospel reading records the Resurrection of Jesus as it was handed onto Matthew. For Matthew, the Resurrection of Jesus is the fulfillment of what Jesus previously promised. Now it was for his followers to go back to Galilee and see him there.

For John of the Cross, the Resurrection was not merely a resuscitation of Jesus' human body but part of God's work to beatify the human race as he did when he created it.

If we have been thus blessed, it behooves us to remember this great work of God because it is easier to see ourselves as clothed in anything but beauty and dignity; and yet this was what Jesus anticipated when he washed the feet of his disciples. He restored them to their original cleanliness and suitability for fellowship with God. Jesus is the model of what fellowship with God looks like. As John says in his Gospel: *no one has ever seen God but the one born of God Jesus Christ.* During the Season of Lent, we saw Jesus fasting (The First Sunday of Lent), in the act of charitable work of healing and caring for the poor (the work of almsgiving), and in prayer (his agony in the Garden). We are invited to do the same but now in the light of having been clothed entirely in the beauty and dignity of Jesus' Resurrection.

PRAYER

Lord God, through your Son's death you destroyed the power of death over us; and through his Resurrection you restored the beauty and dignity in which you created us. Grant, we ask, that we may embrace our own crosses with the same love your Son embraced his cross for our salvation and live in trust of our transformation into your beauty with the same fortitude that your Son gave witness to you. We ask this in Jesus, your Son's name. Amen.

GOSPEL

When the sabbath was over, Mary Magdalene, Mary, the mother of James, and Salome bought spices so that they might go and anoint him. Very early when the sun had risen, on the first day of the week, they came to the tomb. They were saying to one another, "Who will roll back the stone for us from the entrance to the tomb?" When they looked up, they saw that the stone had been rolled back; it was very large. On entering the tomb they saw a young man sitting on the right side, clothed in a white robe, and they were utterly amazed. He said to them, "Do not be amazed! You seek Jesus of Nazareth, the crucified. He has been raised; he is not here. Behold the place where they laid him. "But go and tell his disciples and Peter, 'He is going before you to Galilee; there you will see him, as he told you.'"

M<small>ARK</small> 16: 1-7

ST. JOHN OF THE CROSS

We saw this text on the Third Sunday of Lent in Year B.

"Second, there is detriment to these individuals themselves as to the merit of faith. By giving importance to these miracles one loses the support of the substantial habit of faith, which is an obscure habit. Where signs and testimonies abound, there is less merit in believing. St. Gregory declares that faith is without merit when it has proof from human reason.

"God never works these marvels except when they are a necessity for believing. Lest his disciples go without merit by having sensible proof of his resurrection, he did many things to further their belief before they saw him. Mary Magdalene was first shown the empty sepulcher, and after-

ward the angels told her about the resurrection so she would, by hearing, believe before seeing. As St. Paul says: Faith comes through hearing [Rom 10:17]. And though she beheld him, he seemed only an ordinary man, so by the warmth of his presence he could finish instructing her in the belief she was lacking [Mt 28:1–6; Lk 24:4–10; Jn. 20:11–18]. And the women were sent to tell the disciples first; then these disciples set out to see the sepulcher [Mt 28:7–8]. And journeying incognito to Emmaus with two of his followers, he inflamed their hearts in faith before allowing them to see [Lk 24:15–32]. Finally he reproved all his disciples for refusing to believe those who had told them of his resurrection [Mk 16:14]. And announcing to St. Thomas that they are blessed who believe without seeing, he reprimanded him for desiring to experience the sight and touch of his wounds [Jn 20:25, 29].

"Thus God is not inclined to work miracles. When he works them he does so, as they say, out of necessity. He consequently reprimanded the pharisees because they would not give assent without signs: If you do not see signs and wonders, you do not believe [Jn 4:48]. Those, then, who love to rejoice in these supernatural works suffer a great loss in faith" (A 3.31.8c–9).

REFLECTION

When we think of the Resurrection today, we tend to see it as supplying a faith in Jesus that was not there before he was raised from the dead. You might say the model followed is before: no faith; during: Resurrection; and after: faith. Thus, the Resurrection of Jesus was necessary for faith to take place in the disciples. To a certain extent, this was true. How could the disciples of Jesus have faith in him resurrected from the dead when they were not even sure there was a Resurrection from the dead, let alone not even knowing how to conceive it.

For John of the Cross, however, the Resurrection was not something that supplied a faith that was lacking but rather an event that strengthened the faith they already had. Mary Magdalene, (as a type of all the disciples) had to go through a period of growing in faith before she saw Jesus resurrected from the dead. The disciples had to go through a period of puzzlement and prayer before they could dare think that that empty tomb was a sign of Jesus Risen from the dead. I say "prayer" because the appearance of the angels was an answer to an implicit prayer of Mary Magdalene to cope with an unexpected event. In those days, whenever a person was confronted with something he could not explain, he would pray, or sleep on it and see what a dream would tell him about it. This, in fact, is what happened when Joseph went to sleep troubled about Mary's pregnancy and an angel of the Lord appeared to him to explain the matter.[2]

The work of Christ to build up the faith of his followers so they could "see him risen from the dead" was continued when Christ spoke to his disciples on the way to Emmaus.

While we may be tempted to envy the first disciples because they saw the Risen Lord in a way we cannot, we should remember that they too had to grow in faith both before and after they saw the Risen Lord. Jesus departed from them at his Ascension, and they could have been

---

2. John J. Pilch, *The Cultural World of Jesus: Sunday by Sunday, Cycle A* (Collegeville, MN: The Liturgical Press, 1995), 10–12.

tempted that they had seen an illusion or that they provoked this experience among themselves to make up for the fact that they lost him. Instead, they still believed, even when they no longer saw him and thus experienced him at work in their own lives, in the experience of receiving the Holy Spirit and in the life of the Church.

We, too, received, along with the gift of faith, the gift of the Holy Spirit at Baptism. As we celebrate the event of our Lord's Resurrection, may we avert to him in order to grow in faith and see the Risen Lord at work in our own lives and in the Church.

PRAYER

Lord God, you granted that your Risen Son be seen, not by all, but by those you selected, to bear witness to him. Grant, we ask, that we may grow in the faith they preached and in which we were baptized, so that the merit of our faith may grow before you as we are freed from seeking signs and wonders. We ask this in Jesus' name. Amen.

GOSPEL

At daybreak on the first day of the week the women who had come from Galilee with Jesus took the spices they had prepared and went to the tomb. They found the stone rolled away from the tomb; but when they entered, they did not find the body of the Lord Jesus. While they were puzzling over this, behold, two men in dazzling garments appeared to them. They were terrified and bowed their faces to the ground. They said to them, "Why do you seek the living one among the dead? He is not here, but he has been raised. Remember what he said to you while he was still in Galilee, that the Son of Man must be handed over to sinners and be crucified, and rise on the third day." And they remembered his words. Then they returned from the tomb and announced all these things to the eleven and to all others. The women were Mary Magdalene, Joanna, and Mary the mother of James; the others who accompanied them also told this to the apostles, but their story seemed like nonsense and they did not believe them. But Peter got up and ran to the tomb, bent down, and saw the burial cloths alone; then he went home amazed at what had happened.

LUKE 24: 1-12

ST. JOHN OF THE CROSS

As in the Spiritual Cantical, in the Dark Night of the Soul, John of the Cross writes about the soul searching for [Christ] her beloved.

"We clearly explained this sickness and languor in respect to all things when we mentioned the annihilation of which the soul becomes aware when it begins to climb this ladder of contemplation. It becomes unable then to find satisfaction, support, consolation, or a resting place in anything. The soul therefore begins immediately to ascend from this step to the next.

"The second step causes a person to search for God unceasingly. When the bride said that seeking him by night in her bed (when in accord with the first step of love she was languishing), she did not find him, she added: I will rise up and seek him whom my soul loves [Sg 3:1–2], *which as we said the soul does unceasingly, as David counsels:* Seek the face of God always [Ps 105:4]. *Searching for him in all things, it pays heed to nothing until it finds him. It resembles the bride who, after asking the guards for him, immediately passed by and left them behind [Sg 3:3–4]. Mary Magdalene did not even pay attention to the angels at the sepulcher [Jn 20:14].*

"The soul goes about so solicitously on this step that it looks for its Beloved in all things. In all its thoughts it turns immediately to the Beloved; in all converse and business it at once speaks about the Beloved; when eating, sleeping, keeping vigil, or doing anything else, it centers all its care on the Beloved, as we pointed out in speaking of the anxious longings of love.

"Since the soul is here convalescing and gaining strength in the love found in this second step, it immediately begins to ascend to the third through a certain degree of new purgation in the night, as we will point out, which produces the following effects" (N 2.19.1c–2).

REFLECTION

It is interesting to note that when John of the Cross writes about Mary Magdalene, he often mentions her in the context of the Resurrection. For him, she is the model disciple who does not cease to look for her beloved no matter what is put in her way, whether it be the empty tomb, the disbelief of the disciples, or even angels. She is not satisfied until she finds her Lord for whom she has been looking.

We who have the advantage of hindsight over her may ask ourselves, how often do we seek Jesus? Are we content to find him with a few prayers, an occasional going to Mass, or an occasional reading the Bible?

Do we in turn seek the face of God always or search for him in all things? The feast of the Resurrection is consoling because it reveals Jesus as the Risen One who was once lost through death but now found in his Risen State; but, do we let it rest there? Do we not yet have more work to do to find him in our work, our family, our spouses, and in our hearts?

May the joy of this day inflame us with the desire to be renewed in this search for God. May we not rest until we find him. May we not let anything stand in the way of seeking him with all our heart, our strength, our soul.

PRAYER

Lord God, you filled the hearts of those women: Magdalene, Joanna, and Mary the mother of James, with a great love for your Son. Grant, we ask, that as we celebrate this joyful feast of your Son's Resurrection, we may be blessed with the same love to seek your Son always. We ask this in Jesus, your Son's name. Amen.

EASTER
SUNDAY

GOSPEL

On the first day of the week, Mary of Magdala came to the tomb early in the morning, while it was still dark, and saw the stone removed from the tomb. So she ran and went to Simon Peter and to the other disciple whom Jesus loved, and told them, "They have taken the Lord from the tomb, and we don't know where they put him." So Peter and the other disciple went out and came to the tomb. They both ran, but the other disciple ran faster than Peter and arrived at the tomb first; he bent down and saw the burial cloths there, but did not go in. When Simon Peter arrived after him, he went into the tomb and saw the burial cloths there, and the cloth that had covered his head, not with the burial cloths but rolled up in a separate place. Then the other disciple also went in, the one who had arrived at the tomb first, and he saw and believed. For they did not yet understand the Scripture that he had to rise from the dead.

JOHN 20: 1-9

Alternative readings from Easter Vigil or LUKE 24:13-35
at an afternoon or evening Mass.

ST. JOHN OF THE CROSS

St. John of the Cross describes the spiritual condition that motivates Mary of Magdala to go in search of Christ.

"The soul in this condition of love, then, is like a sick person who is extremely tired and, having lost the taste and appetite for all food, finds it nauseating and everything a disturbance and annoyance. In all that sick people think or see they have only one desire, the desire for health, and everything that does not lead to this is a bother and burden to them.

"Since the soul has reached this sickness of love of God, she has three traits: In all things that are offered to her or with which she deals, she has ever before her that longing for her health, which is her Beloved, and even though she cannot help being occupied with things, she always has her heart fixed on him. The second trait, arising from this first, is the loss of taste for all things. The third, then, which follows from these, is that all these things bother her and all dealings with others are burdensome and annoying.

"The reason for these traits, deduced from what has been said, is that, since the palate of the soul's will has tasted this food of love of God, her will is inclined immediately to seek and enjoy her Beloved in everything that happens and in all her occupations, without looking for any satisfaction or concern of her own. Mary Magdalene acted similarly when with ardent love she was searching for him in the garden. Thinking that he was the gardener, without any further reasoning or consideration she pleaded with him: If you have taken him from me, tell me, and I will take him away [Jn 20:15]. Having a similar yearning to find him in all things, and not immediately finding him as she desires but rather quite the contrary not only does the soul fail to find satisfaction in these things, but they also become a torment to her, and sometimes a very great one. Such souls suffer much in dealing with people and with business matters, for these contacts hinder rather than help them to their goal" (C 10.1–2).

REFLECTION

In today's Gospel, Mary Magdalene goes to the tomb, finding it empty and reporting the absence of Jesus' body to Peter, who in turn runs to the tomb together with the beloved disciple. In Mary Magdalene's love for Jesus, John of the Cross sees a true disciple's love for Jesus. She is the one who was so touched by his love, that she put all things aside to follow him and find him.

Once God touches us through his Son, we can never stop seeking him. This is because God's touch is akin to God himself since he is the one who touches us. It is also because the mystery of Christ is never fully exhausted in one liturgical experience, one liturgical season, or one period of prayer. He is always ever-ancient and ever-new, in the words of St. Augustine.

I hope that during the Season of Lent, you were touched by the Spirit of Christ. Maybe it was not as great as the way John of the Cross describes Mary Magdalene's experience, but enough so that you will continue to seek him in the events of your life, in your relationships, and in your heart.

While we do this searching in a spirit of Easter rejoicing, we also do it in a spirit of longing because until we see him return in glory we will never be fully ourselves. St. Teresa once wrote that God never tires giving himself to us. Thus, let us not tire of receiving him. We do this by searching for him, finding him, giving him back to himself with the same love he has given in himself to us. This circuit of love began with Baptism. May this Season of Easter, built on the asceticism of the Season of Lent, continue this circuit of love of seeking Christ, finding him, and returning him to himself with ourselves.

PRAYER

Lord God, you blessed Mary Magdalene with the grace to seek your Son with a great love after his death. Grant, we ask, that we too may have an equal love for your Son and that we seek him when times are dark and we only have the light of faith to guide us. We ask this in Jesus' name. Amen.

APPENDIX A:
CALENDAR OF LENT 2O1O-2O19
& LECTIONARY CYCLE

Ash Wednesday–Easter

Year	Sunday Year	Lent	Date
2010	C	Ash Wednesday	February 17
		1st Sunday of Lent	February 21
		2nd Sunday of Lent	February 28
		3rd Sunday of Lent	March 7
		4th Sunday of Lent	March 14
		5th Sunday of Lent	March 21
		Palm Sunday	March 28
		Paschal Triduum	April 1
		Easter Sunday	April 4
2011	A	Ash Wednesday	March 9
		1st Sunday of Lent	March 13
		2nd Sunday of Lent	March 20
		3rd Sunday of Lent	March 27
		4th Sunday of Lent	April 3
		5th Sunday of Lent	April 10
		Palm Sunday	April 17
		Paschal Triduum	April 21
		Easter Sunday	April 24

Year	Sunday Year	Lent	Date
2012	B	Ash Wednesday	February 22
		1st Sunday of Lent	February 26
		2nd Sunday of Lent	March 4
		3rd Sunday of Lent	March 11
		4th Sunday of Lent	March 18
		5th Sunday of Lent	March 25
		Palm Sunday	April 1
		Paschal Triduum	April 5
		Easter Sunday	April 8
2013	C	Ash Wednesday	February 13
		1st Sunday of Lent	February 17
		2nd Sunday of Lent	February 24
		3rd Sunday of Lent	March 3
		4th Sunday of Lent	March 10
		5th Sunday of Lent	March 17
		Palm Sunday	March 24
		Paschal Triduum	March 28
		Easter Sunday	March 31

Year	Sunday Year	Lent	Date
2014	A	Ash Wednesday	March 5
		1st Sunday of Lent	March 9
		2nd Sunday of Lent	March 16
		3rd Sunday of Lent	March 23
		4th Sunday of Lent	March 30
		5th Sunday of Lent	April 6
		Palm Sunday	April 13
		Paschal Triduum	April 17
		Easter Sunday	April 20
2015	B	Ash Wednesday	February 18
		1st Sunday of Lent	February 22
		2nd Sunday of Lent	March 1
		3rd Sunday of Lent	March 8
		4th Sunday of Lent	March 15
		5th Sunday of Lent	March 22
		Palm Sunday	March 29
		Paschal Triduum	April 2
		Easter Sunday	April 5

Year	Sunday Year	Lent	Date
2016	C	Ash Wednesday	February 10
		1st Sunday of Lent	February 14
		2nd Sunday of Lent	February 21
		3rd Sunday of Lent	February 28
		4th Sunday of Lent	March 6
		5th Sunday of Lent	March 13
		Palm Sunday	March 20
		Paschal Triduum	March 24
		Easter Sunday	March 27
2017	A	Ash Wednesday	March 1
		1st Sunday of Lent	March 5
		2nd Sunday of Lent	March 12
		3rd Sunday of Lent	March 19
		4th Sunday of Lent	March 26
		5th Sunday of Lent	April 2
		Palm Sunday	April 9
		Paschal Triduum	April 13
		Easter Sunday	April 16

Year	Sunday Year	Lent	Date
2018	B	Ash Wednesday	February 14
		1st Sunday of Lent	February 18
		2nd Sunday of Lent	February 25
		3rd Sunday of Lent	March 4
		4th Sunday of Lent	March 11
		5th Sunday of Lent	March 18
		Palm Sunday	March 25
		Paschal Triduum	March 29
		Easter Sunday	April 1
2019	C	Ash Wednesday	March 6
		1st Sunday of Lent	March 10
		2nd Sunday of Lent	March 17
		3rd Sunday of Lent	March 24
		4th Sunday of Lent	March 31
		5th Sunday of Lent	April 7
		Palm Sunday	April 14
		Paschal Triduum	April 18
		Easter Sunday	April 21

APPENDIX B:
SELECTIONS FROM THE
WRITINGS OF ST. JOHN OF THE CROSS

Ash Wednesday	Ascent of Mount Carmel 3.27.5
Thursday	Ascent of Mount Carmel 2.7.5b
Friday	Ascent of Mount Carmel 2.5.4b
Saturday	Dark Night 2.13.6
1st Sunday A	Ascent 1.5.4–5
1st Sunday B	Dark Night 1.9.5–6
1st Sunday C	Ascent 31.4–5
Monday 1	Ascent 3.30.3–4
Tuesday 1	Ascent of Mount Carmel 3.44.2
Wednesday 1	Ascent of Mount Carmel 2.22.5
Thursday 1	Ascent 2.19.11b–12
Friday 1	Letter 26
Saturday 1	Dark Night 2.20.2
2nd Sunday A	Living Flame of Love 2.25
2nd Sunday B	Living Flame of Love 3.8c–9
2nd Sunday C	Dark Night 2.10.1
Monday 2	Letter 33
Tuesday 2	Counsels to a Religious 5–6
Wednesday 2	Ascent 2.7.6–7a
Thursday 2	Ascent of Mount Carmel 1.4.8
Friday 2	Ascent of Mount Carmel 3.19.7
Saturday 2	Dark Night 1.2.1
3rd Sunday A	Living Flame of Love 1.5–6
3rd Sunday B	Ascent 3.31.8c–9
3rd Sunday C	Ascent of Mount Carmel 1.5.7
Monday 3	Ascent of Mount Carmel 2.7.11
Tuesday 3	Letter 26
Wednesday 3	Letter 19c
Thursday 3	Ascent of Mount Carmel 2.22.6
Friday 3	Dark Night 2.11.4; Sayings 1.47
Saturday 3	Ascent 3.9.1–2

4th Sunday A	Living Flame of Love 3.28–29a
4th Sunday B	Ascent of Mount Carmel 2.5.5
4th Sunday C	Ascent 3.28.1–3
Monday 4	Spiritual Canticle 1.12
Tuesday 4	Dark Night 2.6.3
Wednesday 4	Spiritual Canticle 39.5
Thursday 4	Ascent 3.27.4b–5
Friday 4	Ascent 1.13.2–4
Saturday 4	Living Flame of Love 2.30
5th Sunday A	Spiritual Canticle 2.8
5th Sunday B	Spiritual Canticle 14 &15.10c–e
5th Sunday C	Spiritual Canticle 33.2.2
Monday 5 Years A and B	Dark Night 2.7.3
Monday Year C	Spiritual Canticle 10.6–8
Tuesday 5	Poetry 9.3
Wednesday 5	Spiritual Canticle 22.1
Thursday 5	Living Flame of Love 2.20b–21
Friday 5	Spiritual Canticle 39.5–6
Saturday 5	Ascent 2.19.9c–10
Passion Sunday A	Spiritual Canticle 23.1–2
Passion Sunday B	Spiritual Canticle 23.3–5
Passion Sunday C	Spiritual Canticle 23.6
Monday of Holy Week	Spiritual Canticle 29.10–11
Tuesday of Holy Week	Ascent of Mount Carmel 3.19.8
Wednesday of Holy Week	Dark Night 2.6.3
Chrism Mass	Living Flame of Love 3.26, 28
Holy Thursday	Spiritual Canticle 29.1–2
Good Friday	Ascent 2.7.9–11
Holy Saturday-Vigil Mass A	Spiritual Canticle 5.4
Holy Saturday-Vigil Mass B	Ascent 3.31.8c–9
Holy Saturday-Vigil Mass C	Dark Night 2.19.1c–2
Easter Sunday	Spiritual Canticle 10.1–2

SUGGESTIONS FOR FURTHER READING

ST. JOHN OF THE CROSS

Dicken, E. W. Trueman. *The Crucible of Love: A Study of the Mysticism of St. Teresa of Jesus and St. John of the Cross.* New York: Sheed and Ward, 1963.

Dubay, Thomas. *Fire Within: St. Teresa of Avila, St. John of the Cross, and the Gospel on Prayer.* San Francisco: Ignatius Press, 1989.

Gabriele di Santa Maria Maddalena. *Union with God: According to St. John of the Cross.* Translated by Sister Miriam of Jesus. Eugene OR: Carmel of Maria Regina, 1990.

Herrera, Robert A. Silent Music: *The Life Work and Thought of St. John of the Cross.* Grand Rapids: Eerdmans, 2004.

Howells, Edward. *John of the Cross and Teresa of Avila: Mystical Knowing and Selfhood.* New York: Crossroad, 2002.

Kavanaugh, Kieran. *John of the Cross: Doctor of Light and Love.* Spiritual Legacy Series. New York: Crossroad, 1999.

Matthew, Iain. *The Impact of God: Soundings from St. John of the Cross.* London: Hodder & Stoughton, 1995.

May, Gerald G. *The Dark Night of the Soul: A Psychiatrist Explores the Connection between Darkness and Spiritual Growth.* San Francisco: HarperSanFrancisco, 2004.

Merton, Thomas. *The Ascent to Truth*. New York: Viking Press, 1959.

Moore, Thomas. *Dark Nights of the Soul: A Guide to Finding Your Way through Life's Ordeals*. New York: Gotham Books, 2004.

Muto, Susan Annette. *John of the Cross for Today: The Ascent*. Notre Dame: Ave Maria Press, 1991.

———. *John of the Cross for Today: The Dark Night*. Notre Dame: Ave Maria Press, 1994.

———. *Words of Wisdom for Our World: The Precautions and Counsels of St. John of the Cross*. Preface and translation by Kieran Kavanaugh. Washington, DC: ICS Publications, 1995.

Nemeck, Francis Kelly. *O Blessed Night! Recovering from Addiction Codependency and Attachment Based on the Insights of St. John of the Cross and Pierre Teilhard de Chardin*. New York: Alba House, 1991.

O'Donoghue, Noel. A*dventures in Prayer: Reflections on St. Teresa of Avila, St. John of the Cross, and St. Thérèse of Lisieux*. London: Burns & Oates, 2004.

Peers, E. Allison. *Spirit of Flame: A Study of St. John of the Cross*. Folcroft, PA: Folcroft Library Editions, 1976.

Perrin, David Brian. *For Love of the World: The Old and New Self of John of the Cross*. San Francisco: Catholic Scholars Press, 1997.

St. John of the Cross. *The Collected Works of St. John of the Cross,* rev. ed. Translated by Kieran Kavanaugh, O.C.D. and Otilio Rodriguez, O.C.D. Washington, DC: ICS Publications, 1991.

The quotations herein are from this work.

———. *God Speaks in the Night: The Life, Times, and Teaching of St. John of the Cross*. Translated by Kieran Kavanaugh. Washington DC: ICS Publications, 1991.

CARMELITE SPIRITUALITY

Burrows, Ruth. *Essence of Prayer*. London: Burns & Oates, 2006.

Marie-Eugène de l'Enfant-Jésus, père. *I Want to See God: A Practical Synthesis of Carmelite Spirituality*. Translated by Sister M. Verda Clare. Chicago, Fides Publishers, 1953.

———. *I am a Daughter of the Church: A Practical Synthesis of Carmelite Spirituality*. Translated by Sister M. Verda Clare. Chicago: Fides Publishers, 1955.

McCaffrey, James. *The Carmelite Charism: Exploring the Biblical Roots*. Veritas Publications, 2004.

McGreal, Wilfrid. *At the Fountain of Elijah: The Carmelite Tradition*. Maryknoll, NY: Orbis Books, 1999.

Welch, John. *The Carmelite Way: An Ancient Path for Today's Pilgrim*. New York: Paulist Press, 1996.

INTERNET
RESOURCES

Generalate of the Discalced Carmelite Friars Web site available at
http://www.ocd.pcn.net

Discalced Carmelites Washington Province Web site available at
http://www.ocdwashprov.com/index.htm

Institute of Carmelite Studies Web site available at
http://www.ocdwashprov.com/id33.htm

ICS Publications Web site available at
http://www.icspublications.org

Christus Publishing, LLC Web site available at
http://www.christuspublishing.com

COVER ART

The icon on the cover is a detail from St. John of the Cross by Lynne Taggart, © Lynne Taggart 2000. The icon may be found in the Tabor Carmelite Retreat House, 169 Sharoe Green Lane, Fulwood, Preston, PR2 8HE, United Kingdom. The Web site for Tabor Carmelite Retreat House is available at http://www.tabor-preston.org/.

Ms. Taggart studied painting at Central Saint Martin's School of Art. She has worked on numerous icon commissions and has taught the technique of icon painting for many years. She resides in London where she has a studio. More information about Ms. Taggart and her works may be found on her Web site available at http://freespace.virgin.net/g.ramos-poqui/Lynne/Angels/.

ABOUT THE
AUTHOR

Rev. George Mangiaracina, O.C.D. has been a Discalced Carmelite friar since 1988 with the Discalced Carmelites of the Washington Province. He was ordained into the priesthood in 1993.

He earned a Licentiate degree in Sacred Liturgy in 2001, and his doctorate degree in Sacred Liturgy from Sant' Anselmo College in Rome, Italy in 2008. He has been an adjunct professor at Boston College, where he taught *Exploring Catholicism*. He has written several articles on the Sacred Liturgy. He was born in 1952, in Brooklyn, NY. Currently, he is a conventual member of the Monastery of the Espousal of Mary and Joseph in Brighton, MA.

green press
INITIATIVE

Christus Publishing, LLC is committed to preserving ancient forests and natural resources. We elected to print this title on 30% postconsumer recycled paper, processed chlorine-free. As a result, we have saved:

5 Trees (40' tall and 6-8" diameter)
1 Million BTUs of Total Energy
432 Pounds of Greenhouse Gases
2,079 Gallons of Wastewater
126 Pounds of Solid Waste

Christus Publishing, LLC made this paper choice because our printer, Thomson-Shore, Inc., is a member of Green Press Initiative, a nonprofit program dedicated to supporting authors, publishers, and suppliers in their efforts to reduce their use of fiber obtained from endangered forests.

For more information, visit www.greenpressinitiative.org

Environmental impact estimates were made using the Environmental Defense Paper Calculator. For more information visit: www.edf.org/papercalculator